VIRTUAL WORLD DESIGN AND CREATION FOR TEENS

CHARLES RYAN HARDNETT

Course Technology PTR

A part of Cengage Learning

COURSE TECHNOLOGY
CENGAGE Learning™

Australia • Brazil • Japan • Korea • Mexico • Singapore • Spain • United Kingdom • United States

COURSE TECHNOLOGY
CENGAGE Learning™

Virtual World Design and Creation for Teens
Charles Ryan Hardnett

**Publisher and General Manager,
Course Technology PTR:** Stacy L. Hiquet

Associate Director of Marketing: Sarah Panella

Manager of Editorial Services: Heather Talbot

Marketing Manager: Jordan Casey

Acquisitions Editor: Heather Hurley

Project/Copy Editor: Kezia Endsley

Technical Editor: Parker Hiquet

Teen Reviewer: Erin Daily

PTR Editorial Services Coordinator: Jen Blaney

Interior Layout Tech: Macmillan Publishing
Solutions

CD-ROM Producer: Brandon Penticuff

Cover Designer: Mike Tanamachi

Proofreader: Tonya Cupp

Indexer: Sharon Shock

For product information and technology assistance, contact us at
Cengage Learning Customer & Sales Support, 1-800-354-9706

For permission to use material from this text or product, submit all requests online at **www.cengage.com/permissions**
Further permissions questions can be emailed to
permissionrequest@cengage.com

Xbox is a registered trademark of Microsoft Corporation in the United States and/or other countries.
PlayStation is a registered trademark of the Sony Corporation.

All other brand names and product names mentioned in this book are trademarks or service marks of their respective companies. Any omission or misuse (of any kind) of service marks or trademarks should not be regarded as intent to infringe on the property of others. The publisher recognizes and respects all marks used by companies, manufacturers, and developers as a means to distinguish their products.

Library of Congress Control Number: 2008936199

ISBN-13: 978-1-59863-850-9

ISBN-10: 1-59863-850-5

Course Technology, a part of Cengage Learning
20 Channel Center Street
Boston, MA 02210
USA

Cengage Learning is a leading provider of customized learning solutions with office locations around the globe, including Singapore, the United Kingdom, Australia, Mexico, Brazil, and Japan. Locate your local office at: **international.cengage.com/region**

Cengage Learning products are represented in Canada by Nelson Education, Ltd.

For your lifelong learning solutions, visit **courseptr.com**

Visit our corporate website at **cengage.com**

Printed in the United States of America
1 2 3 4 5 6 7 12 11 10 09

Acknowledgments

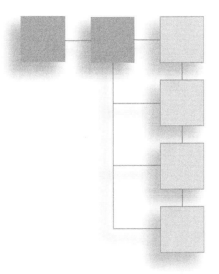

I'd like to acknowledge all of the people associated with Course Technology who helped to make the book a reality. I thank them for their patience with a first-time book author. I thank them for the encouragement, feedback, hard work, and diligence. I look forward to future endeavors. In particular, I thank Heather Hurley for giving me this opportunity, and Kezia Endsley, for her guidance throughout the process and for her awesome editing.

I especially thank Erin Daily, a CARE Camp student and camp volunteer counselor, who served as teen reviewer for this book. Her comments and feedback were invaluable.

My greatest thanks goes to my wife, Felicia, for her encouragement and understanding through the long nights of writing. She helped to keep me going during the toughest times. I also thank my children for letting Daddy work on this book at times when they wanted to play. I love you!

ABOUT THE AUTHOR

Charles R. Hardnett is a professor in the Computer Science Department at Spelman College. His areas of specialty include high-performance languages and compilers, operating systems, embedded systems, computer networks, and computer graphics/gaming. He has published research articles in the areas of high-performance languages and compilers, embedded systems, computer networks, and computer science education. Currently, he teaches a computer graphics course themed in game design that targets college junior and senior Computer Science majors. This course teaches students the principles of computer graphics as they learn to build computer games for PCs and Xbox 360 consoles. In addition, Prof. Hardnett is developing a Game Design program at Spelman College for students interested in careers in digital gaming or digital animation careers. Furthermore, Prof. Hardnett has designed and taught programming courses covering a wide variety of programming languages, including C++ and Java. He has also developed courses entitled Discovering Computer Science, Embedded Systems Compilers and Architecture Design, Operating Systems, Programming Language Design and Implementation, Computer Networks, Compiler Design and Implementation, and Data Structures and Algorithms.

Prof. Hardnett is also the director of the CARE (Computer And Robotics Education) Summer Computer Camp for Computer Graphics and Robotics (www.spelman.edu/~care/CARE/Camp.html). His summer camp targets middle school students in the Metro-Atlanta area. The camp is a vehicle to introduce students to Computer Science using Alice for the computer graphics and animation and Sony AIBO or Lego Mindstorms for the robotics.

Prof. Hardnett is the son of Charles and Bernice Hardnett. He inherited his love of teaching from his father, a retired college basketball coach, and his mother, a retired high school teacher. Prof. Hardnett is married to Felicia Hardnett and they have two children, Erin and Charles, Jr. (CJ). He and his family currently reside in a suburb of Atlanta, GA.

Contents

INTRODUCTION

Hello World! This is meant to be a book that you can use to learn and have fun while you learn how to create virtual worlds. Virtual worlds are found in video games, websites, and animated movies. I have taught the contents of this book to teens and tweens for several years. Most of the students I teach at this level have some exposure to virtual worlds; they use them when playing games, for example. However, most of my students have no previous experience with creating virtual worlds or programming a computer. I always have a great time watching the students start from not knowing how to do any computer programming to acquiring the ability and confidence to create a computer program. When you go from being a user to a creator or programmer, you experience a truly exciting dimension of computers.

You can now learn how to create software that will entertain and/or be useful to others. You can then take your ideas and make them a reality. Imagine saying to yourself, "I wish this software/program could do…", where you fill in the blank with some special feature that you think would be very useful. When you become a programmer, you could actually make that feature yourself! That is an awesome feeling. This book is a great first step on the journey to becoming a creator and not just a user.

Creating a virtual world requires that you program the computer in a special way. So I am going to share some of my thoughts on computer programming. Programming a computer is one of the most satisfying activities I can imagine. Growing up, I was always interested in how something worked, whether it was a radio, camera, cassette player, CD player, car, or computer. So this usually meant having to take apart the camera with a screwdriver and other tools. It was really fun discovering what was underneath the external plastic shell. Each time I took something off, I would find another part underneath. I'd see what happens when buttons were pushed or knobs were turned. I would see how the lens of the camera was attached. I usually would consult an encyclopedia to help me recognize the parts and what they were used for. Each part of the camera had a role, and each part was essential to giving the camera its features.

When I first started learning about software, it was a very similar experience. Software does not require screwdrivers and pliers to open it. When you open software to see what is inside, you reveal its program. A computer program is a set of special instructions that is understood by the computer. These instructions tell the computer what to do. For example, there are sets of instructions that tell the computer how to execute the word-processing program called Word. These instructions tell the computer to show a splash screen first. Then these instructions tell the computer how to create a window, menu, icons, and so on. The instructions tell the computer how to drop down a menu when the user clicks on it, and how to perform the operation such as opening a file when the user selects that from the menu. A computer programmer writes these instructions. A computer programmer is someone who has learned one or more computer programming languages and uses those languages to program computers.

A computer programming language looks a lot like English mixed with some mathematical symbols. Some languages use words like `if`, `while`, and `then`, with math symbols such as ( ), +, /, and =. When you learn how to use the instructions of a programming language, you can create very interesting and exciting programs. You can also look at programs that were written by other people and learn how they work or even modify the programs to do something special for you.

The Philosophy of This Book

This book was written with the typical student in mind. Students who decide they want to learn about virtual worlds typically ask questions such as "How do I start?", "How do I move my person in the world?", and "I like sound, so how do I add sound to my world?". These questions are typically difficult to answer with a standard computer-programming book that is organized by the features of the language rather than by the tasks the programmer would like to perform.

For example, if you wanted to know how to make a person move around the world, in a traditional programming book you would have to know that you need something called a library that contains special commands to program your keyboard or mouse. You would have to find that information in the book first. Then you would need to know that you have to find the special commands that allow you to just move a character. You would have to find those commands in the book. Then you would have to take what you have uncovered from these different parts of the book and put it together to make it so the user could move the character around the world. However, in this book, you can just go to the chapter that discusses how to move the main character around the world. This chapter brings together the content from the two chapters of a traditional programming book into one chapter to show you how to achieve that goal. This philosophy works well because this book is about programming virtual worlds, and not just about programming computers.

Because the topic is more focused, the book can be presented in a customized way to address the issues you will face with building virtual worlds. And on the way, you will learn how to program computers, and have lots of fun.

How to Use This Book

This book is best read in sequential order, chapter by chapter. In the first few chapters, you will begin thinking about ideas for the project you would like to build. As you complete the exercises in a chapter, you should think about your own project. Once you have completed the chapter exercises, you should try to apply the ideas to your project. Therefore, as you work through the book, you will be creating your own project. For those who have trouble coming up with a project, there are some project ideas on the accompanying CD in the Starting Points folder.

To effectively use this book, you should sit at the computer with Alice (www.alice.org) as you read the book. You should read and then follow the steps from the book using Alice. In other words, you should be active while reading this book. This is how you will learn best.

Resources for Help

There are several resources for helping you if you get stuck. First, you should always double-check the instructions to make sure that you did not miss a step or misunderstand a step if your result is not what you were expecting. Second, you will find the exercises from the book on the CD in completed form. Sometimes it helps to see the finished product to understand it, and then try it on your own. Third, the software used in this book is called Alice. Alice has a forum that you can join online. The online forum is a place where you can post questions and other Alice creators will be able to respond to your questions and help you. Fourth, you have the website for this book, which contains good, updated information that may be helpful to you as well as other exercises and examples. The website is www.spelman.edu/~hardnett/vworlds. Finally, take advantage of friends and family. Even if they are not familiar with Alice, sometimes it helps to explain your problem to other people to determine how to fix it.

Using the CD

The accompanying CD contains solutions and other examples as well as some starting points. The CD has a folder for each chapter, which contains the solutions and examples from that chapter. You can look at these files if you get stuck, or if you lose your work and don't want to start over. There is one folder called *Starting Points* that is provided to help you come up with a project of your own. When you open an Alice project from this folder you will see information in the program that gives you an idea for a story. You can use that story as a jumping off point for your own story. The initial scenes are already set up for you so you can start programming your game or movie.

Book Summary

You'll find the following chapters in this book:

- Chapter 1: Provides background information on virtual worlds and how they are used.

- Chapter 2: Explains how to create stories, which is how you start any virtual world project.

- Chapter 3: Introduces you to the software program called Alice that is used to build the virtual worlds in this book.

- Chapter 4: Explains how you create the start of your virtual world. You will learn how to set up the scene with different scenery objects.

- Chapter 5: Explains how you allow the users to control your main character.

- Chapter 6: Explains how you can have the computer move characters for you. Some of these ideas can also be applied to your main character.

- Chapter 7: Where you will learn to detect collisions between characters in your world. This is fundamental to being able to create games.

- Chapter 8: Shows you how to add multiple scenes to your world to make them more interesting. In games, these scenes can be levels.

- Chapter 9: Discusses adding sounds to your worlds.

- Chapter 10: Teaches you how to keep score, which is very important in games but can be used in other situations as well.

- Chapter 11: Teaches you how to add finishing touches to your world by showing you how to add title screens and scrolling credits.

- Chapter 12: Teaches you how to add more sophistication to your world by making characters aware of each other and allowing them to chase or run away from each other.

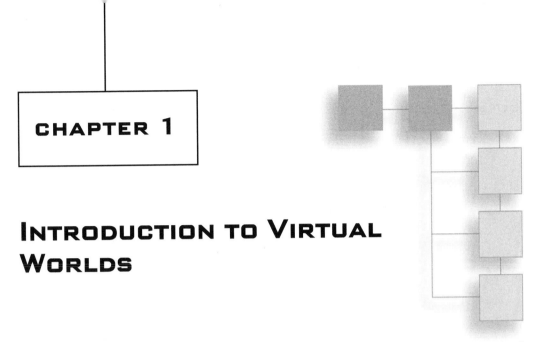

CHAPTER 1

INTRODUCTION TO VIRTUAL WORLDS

Have you ever wondered about how video games are made? Have you watched an animated movie and wondered "How do they do that?" If you answered yes to these questions, you are in the right place. This is the beginning of a journey into the development of computer video games, animated movies, and other forms of computer graphics entertainment. The common thread for all of these genres of computer graphics entertainment is the virtual world. In this chapter, several questions will be answered, including:

- What is a virtual world?

- How are virtual worlds used in movies?

- How are virtual worlds used in social networks?

- How are virtual worlds used in games?

Understanding Virtual Worlds

The term *virtual world* has several definitions. The term virtual world is portrayed as a new concept in the popular media and it has a very narrow meaning to describe online social networks such as *Second Life* and *Club Penguin*. After you read this chapter, you will understand that this concept was introduced many decades ago and has a broad application. This is why there are several definitions.

You can search online for definitions, and you will see the variety of responses. Here are a few example definitions found online:

> A *virtual world* is a computer-based simulated environment intended for its users to inhabit and interact via avatars.—Wikipedia.org

> A *virtual world* is a computer-generated, three-dimensional representation of a setting within which the users of the technology perceive themselves to be and within which interaction takes place; also called virtual landscape, virtual space, and virtual environment.—Dictionary.com

> A *virtual world* is an extension of our real world that exists only online; i.e. the cyber world—www.osixs.net

This list of examples demonstrates that there is no single accepted definition. If you do your own search, you will even find that the definitions seem to change, as people understand more. However, you can learn from these definitions that a virtual world has something to do with computers, it is not real, and it feels like the real world. In this book, we will use this definition:

Virtual world, noun, a computer-generated world that contains simulated characters and scenery objects. This definition is a simple and flexible definition for a virtual world. The characters will be people, animals, aliens, monsters, or any other creature that moves, talks, and so on. The scenery objects can be furniture, trees, flowers, grass, dirt, hills, and so on. This definition is more flexible because it allows a virtual world to exist online or offline. In addition, this definition allows a virtual world to look like the real world or be an imaginary world. Finally, this definition does not require anyone to interact with the virtual world.

Figure 1.1 shows an example of Pac-Man. This is a 2D arcade game that has a very simple virtual world. In this world the characters are the ghosts and the Pac-Man. The scenery objects include the pellets (small dots), power pellets (large dots in the corners), the maze, the tunnel, and the small prizes. You should see that this world is computer generated and contains the characters and objects; and thus it fits the definition for a virtual world.

The screen shot shown in Figure 1.2 is interesting for several reasons. First, it is an example of a 3D virtual world. Second, it is from a virtual reality software package that is meant to help the user drive a car more effectively and safely. There are scenery objects such as the roads, trees, grass, and clouds.

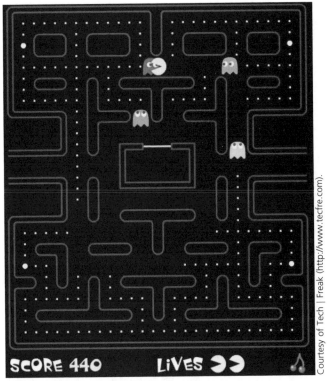

Courtesy of Tech | Freak (http://www.tecfre.com).

Figure 1.1
A screen shot from the game Pac-Man that illustrates how simple a virtual world can be.

Courtesy of the Virtual Reality Laboratory at the Olin
Neuropsychiatry Research Center at the Institute of Living
(www.nrc-iol.org/cores/index.htm)

Figure 1.2
A screen shot from a driving-simulation software that illustrates a simple three-dimensional virtual world.

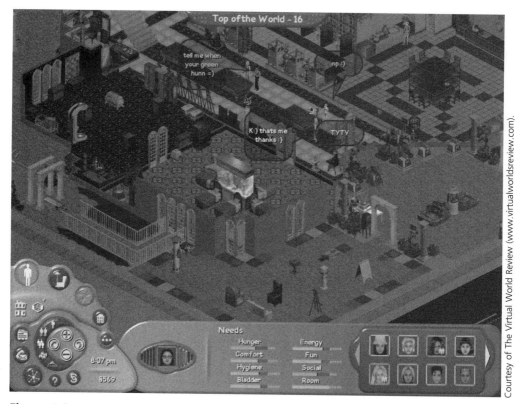

Figure 1.3
A screen shot from the popular *The Sims* series of games that illustrates a complex three-dimensional virtual world.

There are also characters such as the cars and the person crossing the street. Again, you should see that this meets the definition of a virtual world: it contains computer-generated scenery and characters.

Figure 1.3 shows a more complex 3D virtual world that is found in a popular online version of *The Sims*. This 3D virtual world contains numerous people and animals (fish in the fish tank), which are all characters. The virtual world also contains lots of scenery objects that provide a detailed virtual world.

Now that you have a good idea what a virtual world is, let's learn about common ways in which virtual worlds are used in the real world.

How Virtual Worlds Are Used in Movies

Do you enjoy watching animated movies? What are some of your favorite animated movies? Some of my favorites include *Cars, Shrek, Finding Nemo,* and *WALL-E.* These are examples of animated movies that were created with the use

Courtesy of Pixar Corporation (www.pixar.com).

Figure 1.4
A screen shot with a character from the movie *Up*.

Courtesy of Pixar Corporation (www.pixar.com).

Figure 1.5
A scenic screen shot from the movie *Up*.

of computer graphics and computer animation. Figures 1.4 and 1.5 show screen shots from the Disney/Pixar movie *Up*. These scenes are computer generated and represent parts of the virtual world created for the movie. Figure 1.4 shows a character from the movie arriving to a home with a fence. Figure 1.5 shows a nature scene of a valley filled with trees.

The computer graphics are used to create the characters and scenery in these movies. The scenery is the virtual world where the movie takes place. In these examples from the movie *Up*, the virtual world has a city scene and a wilderness scene. In the case of *Finding Nemo*, this virtual world primarily was an undersea world. There are colorful coral reefs, caverns, sunken ships, and other objects that

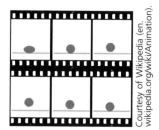

Courtesy of Wikipedia (en. wikipedia.org/wiki/Animation).

Figure 1.6
Six frames for an animated bouncing ball.

you will find undersea. In the case of *Cars*, the scenery includes the race tracks where the races took place and all of the scenery objects found there, and the entire small western town and all of its buildings, the main road, and mountains. The characters in *Finding Nemo* are primarily sea creatures, including fish, sharks, whales, and sea turtles. The characters in *Cars* are various vehicles such as racing cars, trucks, and other cars. The animation is where characters and other objects in the movie are moving. Computers do the animation in these movies.

Before computer animation, artists drew the animation. An animation is composed of several still pictures or drawings called a *frame*. Each frame shows a small change in the scene so that when they are put together in the proper sequence and at the proper speed, the characters will appear to be moving. In a typical film, the frames must move at a rate of at least 24 frames per second, and therefore a one-hour movie would require 86,400 frames (60 × 60 × 24) at the very minimum. It is easy to see why this would be a very tedious process, and you can also see why computer animation would save a lot of time. However, before talking more about computer animation, let's dive a little deeper into traditional hand-drawn animation so that you can understand it better.

Figure 1.6 shows an example of animation frames. These frames show a ball bouncing. If the frames are viewed in order, the ball will appear to bounce up and down. In frame 1, the ball is compressed. As the ball decompresses in frames 2 and 3, it gets thicker and lifts off the ground. In frame 4, the ball reaches its highest peak, and in frames 6 and 7, the ball returns to the floor. Repeating frame 1 would continue the animation. The following exercise gives you a chance to create your own animation and have some first-hand experience.

Exercise: Creating a Flipbook

It's time to see what it is like to make your own animation. This exercise shows you how animation is organized and is also an introduction to developing animated movies and video games using storyboards. A flipbook is where you place each step of the animation on a page of

THE KINEOGRAPH.

Courtesy of Wikipedia (en.wikipedia.org/wiki/Flipbook).

Figure 1.7
A typical flipbook animation.

the book. For example, if you wanted to put the animation of Figure 1.6 into a flipbook, each frame of the animation would be drawn on a separate page. You would then be able to flip the pages with your thumb and it will appear that the ball is actually bouncing. This exercise will step you through the process of creating a flipbook of the bouncing ball animation. An example of a flipbook is shown in Figure 1.7.

Materials needed:

■ Several sheets of 8.5 × 11-inch paper

■ Pair of scissors (optional)

■ Stapler or binder clip

■ Black colored pencil

Instructions:

1. Make guidelines on a sheet of paper, as shown in Figure 1.8.

2. Make a small stack of paper with the guideline sheet on top. Cut all the sheets with the scissors using the lines as a guide. If you have too many sheets, cut fewer sheets at a time.

3. Repeat Steps 1 and 2 until you have a nice set of pages; approximately 20 pages is a good start.

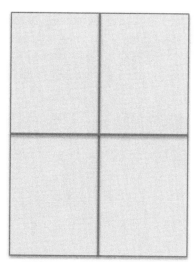

Figure 1.8
Sheet of paper divided into four pages to be cut by scissors.

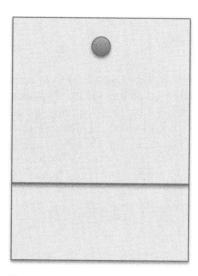

Figure 1.9
Shows the first frame on the last page with the ball at its starting point.

4. Draw a picture of a ball at the top of the last page of the book, as shown in Figure 1.9.
   Draw the ground at about two-thirds of the way down the page.

5. On the next to last page draw another picture of the ball moved slightly down (about half
   the height of a ball). This is shown in Figure 1.10. The dotted ball shows where in
   relationship from its old position the new ball should be. Do not draw the dotted ball. Don't
   forget to draw the ground again.

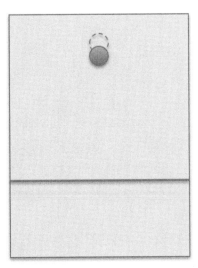

Figure 1.10
Shows the second frame on the next to last page with the ball moved down from its original position.

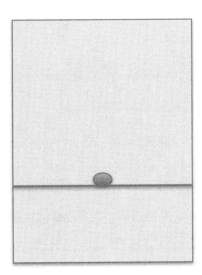

Figure 1.11
The compressed ball hitting the ground.

6. Continue drawing the ball moving downward on each page until you have drawn about nine frames (one per page) or until you are about one frame from the ground.

7. When the ball hits the ground it will compress, and so draw it as an oval touching the ground. This is shown in Figure 1.11.

Figure 1.12
The ball decompressing as it rebounds upward.

8. On the next frame, draw the ball up from its last position with less of an oval shape. This is shown in Figure 1.12. Lessening the oval shape gives the perception that the ball is decompressing back to normal shape.

9. Continue drawing the slight oval moving up for about two more frames, and then continue drawing a normal circle going up until you have reached the starting point or until you have run out of pages. Your last frame should look similar to your first frame.

Flip through your book using your thumb as shown in Figure 1.7 and you have made your first animation.

You should experiment with making other animations. You could draw a spinning box, a stick figure running, and so on. Have some fun with flipbooks.

Imagine if you had to do over 86,000 of these sheets!! This gives you some idea of what a cartoonist has to do to create a traditional animated cartoon.

However, in today's world most animated film for television and the theatre are generated with the use of computers. The computers help generate these animated movies in several ways. There is software that artists/cartoonists can use to create animation and there is software that requires the skills of a computer programmer. The software that artists use is called *modeling software*. Modeling software allows the artists to draw characters and scenery objects on the computer and combine them to create a scene of the movie.

The animation of the characters is done by what is known as *key-frame animation*. In key-frame animation the artist creates the first and last frame of the animation sequence of the character or perhaps the first, middle, and last frame of the animation. The computer software will fill in the missing frames to obtain a smooth animation. Examples of this type of software are 3D Studio Max and Maya.

The second technique is where an artist creates a programmable character called a computer model. In fact, the same software used in the previous method is used for creating this computer model. A group of programmers creates a computer program or software that plays the movie. This program loads the computer models created by the artists. The computer model can be controlled by instructions in the program. For example, there are instructions that can move the character's legs or the character's arms. Therefore, putting the instructions in the right order programs the model to appear to be walking.

Both techniques are used in complementary ways in today's featured animated film. Artist can do the simpler movements with the modeling software, whereas the more complex movements are programmed. The virtual worlds created for animated movies rely on techniques that are similar to those used in creating virtual worlds for social networks.

How Virtual Worlds Are Used in Social Networks

Social networks have become an international pastime for teens and adults. There are some social networks such as Facebook and MySpace that allow people to send messages, share photographs, share video, and post blogs to friends, families, and other acquaintances. These social networks are typically based on real-life experiences in the real world and serve as a way of sharing those experiences.

However, another type of social network is becoming more and more popular. This second type of social network is based on virtual worlds, where people can create a "virtual life" that mimics the activities and interactions of the real world. These virtual world social networks resemble the video game series based on The Sims. However, these virtual worlds are played online in a social network, and each avatar in these virtual worlds is meant to represent an actual user. Figure 1.13 shows one such online social network called *Second Life*.

Figure 1.13
A landscape screen shot from *Second Life* that shows the level of realism and fantasy.

An *avatar* is a computer user's representation of himself/herself; most commonly thought of as a three-dimensional character used in computer games. Avatars may also be two-dimensional like those found in instant messaging programs such as Yahoo Instant Messenger or textual representations such as those used in early chat rooms of the 1980s and 90s. In a virtual world social network, you can move the avatar, make decisions for the avatar, and customize its appearance. The avatar in the virtual world typically does things that people do in the real world. For example, an avatar may walk around and explore the virtual world or an avatar may strike up a conversation with another avatar. In some virtual worlds, such as *Second Life* (see Figure 1.14), avatars may own land and build buildings on their property and have careers. Or the avatar may be going to college and have a roommate in a shared apartment.

The avatars in these social network worlds, as shown in Figures 1.14 and 1.15, can be moved and manipulated by the users once they have logged into the virtual

Figure 1.14
Avatars from *Second Life*. These avatars are at a dance club. You can see the different characteristics of the avatars and how personalized they are and you can see the detail of the world.

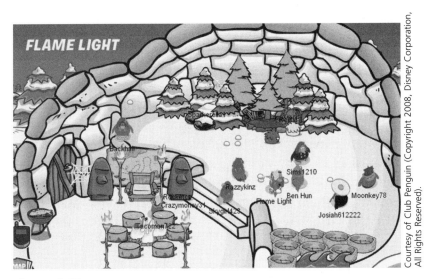

Figure 1.15
Avatars from *Club Penguin*. These avatars are fantasy avatars in a fantasy world. Each user is a penguin in *Club Penguin*. The igloo shown here is a favorite hangout spot in *Club Penguin*. You can see the personalization of the avatars.

world. Each virtual world has its own way of moving characters. However, a human player does not control some avatars in the virtual world. These avatars are affectionately known as "bots," and are controlled by a computer program. These avatars incorporate artificial intelligence or A.I. to give the appearance to other users that human players are actually controlling them. In most of these social network virtual worlds it's fairly easy to pick out which avatars are "bots". This is because the A.I. that is used for most of these avatars is not very advanced. Two popular examples of these worlds where you can interact with avatars are *Teen Second Life* and *Club Penguin*.

Now let's will explore how these types of virtual worlds are created. First, there is a need for artists who can draw the avatars, the scenery, and the other objects. The same types of software used by artists in animated movies are used here for designing avatars and other objects. Secondly, just like in animated movies, the characters have to be programmed to move. However, there are some significant differences between social networks and animated movies. In these social network virtual worlds, you can move the characters to explore the world and you have the ability to make decisions about what the characters do and how they look. These two ideas are what we call *interactivity*. So a social network virtual world has interactivity, whereas an animated movie virtual world does not.

Another way of looking at interactivity is that it allows users to change the story of their characters! In an animated movie, the story is preset and you are watching the story unfold as it was planned and produced. However, in a social network virtual world, users actually develop the story by interacting with their characters. In addition, a movie has a definite ending, but these social network virtual worlds do not have an ending. Your story is just part of the larger story and even when you stop playing, the stories of other characters continue! Interactivity is accomplished by programming computers to interact using the keyboard and mouse. The computer is programmed to respond to your choices and selections as you make them. Your actions can affect your avatar, other avatars, or objects in the virtual world. This is the work of computer programmers.

Social network virtual worlds are similar to those used in animated films. The worlds are filled with scenery objects as well as characters. However, you can interact with a social network virtual world and you become a part of the story. You have an affect on the story in the social network virtual world. In fact, users in the virtual world have their own story to create very much like real life. In addition, you can customize your avatar's look and behaviors. The interactivity and accumulation of assets that you have in a social network virtual world is similar to a video game. In the next section, you'll read about virtual worlds in video games.

Visit the following websites:

Second Life at http://teen.secondlife.com/.

Club Penguin at http://www.clubpenguin.com/.

Do the following short exercises:

1. List some characteristics that you would choose for your avatar. A characteristic is something that affects the avatar's appearance such as the skin color.

2. List some activities that you can do with your avatar. An activity is action that your avatar can perform. In *Second Life,* shopping is one such activity; you should come up with some others.

3. List three goals for your avatar. A goal is an accomplishment you would like for your avatar to achieve. In *Club Penguin* you can earn points to purchase outfits for your avatar. Choose some goals that you would like for your avatar to accomplish.

4. List two ways that these social network virtual worlds are similar to animated movies and shows.

5. List two ways that these social network virtual worlds are different from animated movies and shows.

How Virtual Worlds Are Used in Games

Computer video games have become one of the most profitable sectors of the entertainment industry because people are playing more computer video games now than ever in history. The gaming sector has earned more money than the movie and music industry in recent years, and this trend is expected to continue. At the center of computer video games are virtual worlds. I am sure that you enjoy playing computer video games on your PC, Macintosh, Xbox, PlayStation, Wii, or one of the other many devices that have computer video games. What are some of your favorite games? Do you like *The Sims, Madden Football, Halo, Wii Sports,* or *Zuma*?

The basis of a computer video game is the virtual world where the game takes place. In some games the virtual world is an elaborate world such as in *The Sims* or *Halo,* the virtual world may be confined to a small area such as a football field like in *Madden Football,* or the virtual world can be a basic background like in *Pong* or *Tetris.* Virtual worlds in games can be made to resemble the real world or can be a fantasy world. Fantasy worlds are typically created more in computer video games than in animated movies and social network virtual worlds. For example, *Tetris* has a virtual world that does not resemble any real-world situation where you are in a room with blocks falling out of the sky and you have to stack them by turning and flipping them and moving them left and right until they land on a heap of blocks. Likewise, the virtual world in *Halo* is a depiction of a future version of Earth or another planet inhabited by humans. The scenery resembles some of what we experience in real life, but it is obvious that this computer video game does not take place in today's world.

As with animated movies and social network virtual worlds, there are different characters in computer video games. In computer video games you have the primary character(s), which are controlled by you and your friends when you play the game. You also have supporting avatars, which are characters that may be enemy characters, background characters, or other teammates that are not controlled by humans. The supporting characters can be sorted into two categories based on how they are controlled:

- Indirect human control

- Computer control

The *indirect human control* type of supporting character performs actions based on your instructions, but a computer carries out the actions. Examples of these types of characters are the players on your football team. You call the play for your team to execute, and you control one of the players on the team. The other 10 players execute the play that you called, but it's the computer that actually makes them run the play. Once the play starts, you do not directly control the actions of the other 10 players. They do execute the play you have selected, so you have some loose control over their behavior.

The *computer-controlled* supporting player is one that is completely controlled by the computer. An example of these types of characters is the opposing team in the football game when you are playing against the computer. In this case, the computer calls the offensive and defensive plays for the opposing team. The computer also executes the play by making the players of the opposing team perform the required actions. You do not have any control over the player's actions on the opposing team.

In computer video games it is becoming common that you can create an avatar that is in your likeness. Just like with social network virtual worlds, you can customize the appearance of your avatar. You can change everything about its physical appearance including the height, body type, facial features, skin complexion, and clothing to name a few of the options. However, there are other characteristics that are typically found in some computer video games such as the player's speed, strength, and quickness. These are characteristics typically found in action and sports games.

A single person or a team of people can develop computer video games. A team usually consists of producers, directors, writers, financial managers, marketers, artists, musicians, and computer programmers:

- The producers are responsible for managing the process of developing the game, which goes through several stages.

- The directors direct the action in the games and help to develop the scenes and determine how the characters should move in the scenes.

- The writers are responsible for developing the background story and dialogue used in the game; you will read more about storytelling in Chapter 2.

- The financial managers are responsible for making sure the project has the money to be completed. The money is used to pay for every aspect of the development, manufacturing, packaging, advertising, and distribution of the game.

- The marketers are responsible for developing the television and magazine advertisements for the game.

- The musicians create, arrange, and mix the music and sound effects of the game.

- The artists are responsible for drawing and modeling the environment of the game including the scenery and objects, which are built using the same techniques they used for animated movies and social network virtual worlds. The artists also create the characters found in the games. These characters are created using the same software tools that were used for the animated movies and the social network virtual worlds.

In computer games the computer programmers program the models created by the artists. The models are programmed because computer video games are very interactive. The interactivity makes it impossible to predict the behavior and the actions of the characters when the artists are drawing them. Programmers use programming languages such as C/C++ or Java to program the characters to be controlled by the game pads, the keyboard, the mouse, or other input devices. In addition, the programmers must program the indirect and computer-controlled characters to act appropriately. The programmers use A.I. to make these characters chase other characters, run away from other characters, to make decisions during a conversation with another character, or any other activity that gives them a perceived intelligence.

Exercise: Exploring Computer Games

This exercise helps you explore the virtual worlds of some of your favorite games. You need to pick at least two games. One of the games should have a simple virtual world, such as Pac-Man shown in Figure 1.1, and the other game a more complex virtual world, such as *The Sims* shown in Figure 1.3. Make a table like this one for each of the games:

Scenery Objects	Human-Controlled Characters	Computer-Controlled Characters

You will examine the virtual worlds for your two games and identify the scenery objects that found in these games. Write the names of those objects and some of their characteristics in parentheses in the first column. Do the same for human controlled characters and computer controlled characters in the second and third columns. Here is an example using Pac-Man (Refer to Figure 1.1 if you do not recall Pac-Man).

Scenery Objects	Human-Controlled Characters	Computer-Controlled Characters
The maze (blue thin lines) The ghost box (blue lines with a white door) Power pellets (large white circles) Regular pellets (small white dots) Bonus food (cherries, strawberry, pretzel, and so on)	The Pac-Man (yellow)	The four ghosts (light blue, red, orange, and pink; some are fast and some are slow; they know how to chase Pac-Man)

Summary

In this chapter, you were introduced to virtual worlds. You explored how virtual worlds are used in animated movies, social network virtual worlds, and computer video games. You were able to see that there are similarities in these virtual worlds as well as differences. You also could see that there are several types of people needed to create animated movies, social network virtual worlds, and computer video games. These people include artists, computer programmers, writers, and so on. Now with this introduction to virtual worlds, your next step is to learn about how animated movies, social network virtual worlds, and computer video games are designed.

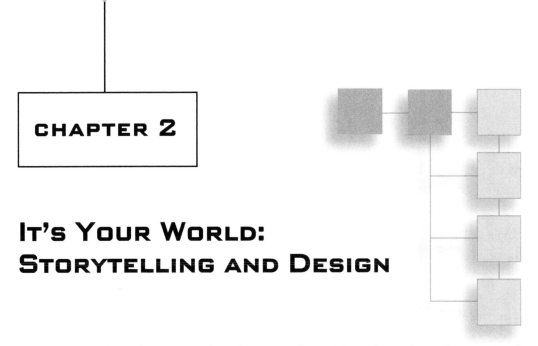

CHAPTER 2

It's Your World: Storytelling and Design

Now that you have been introduced to virtual worlds and seen how they are used in various media, this chapter focuses on showing you how to build your own virtual worlds for short movies and/or computer video games. Movies and computer video games have a process that is followed when creating them. Each of the processes has important differences; however, they are remarkably similar in many aspects. Because of their similarity, I will show you a process that can be used for both where you shift the emphasis of work in the various stages depending on your goal of creating an animated movie or a video game.

The process I will present to you is an introductory process. If you were to pursue becoming a movie producer or director then you would learn a more detailed process than what is used here. Likewise, if you were to become a video game designer or producer, you would learn a different, but equally detailed, process for developing a video game. Near the beginning of each of these processes is the need to develop a conceptual basis for the game. In this book, the concept is called the *story*.

Developing a Good Story

Why do you need a story when designing video games? You could argue that all games do not have a story, and games are very successful without a story. However, in the context of games competing with movies in the marketplace and the sophistication of the technology used for games it is almost a necessity to have a story at the heart of the game. A story provides a way for the person playing your game to have an emotional attachment to the game or the characters. If the players of the game become emotionally attached to the game, they will more likely continue to play the game and its sequels. I have seen this phenomenon with my own children. They enjoy playing sports games, driving games, action games, and so on. However, the games that they are most intrigued by and play the longest are the games where there is a compelling story.

Sometimes the video game story is based on other media such as a movie or television show. In other cases, the story was developed strictly for the game. I hear my kids talking about the characters in the game as if they are actual people. They want to see the characters succeed because they care about the characters and the story in which the character lives. I will say more about this later.

Storytelling is a vast and deep collection of concepts, skills, and knowledge. This book will only tap into a very small amount of this knowledge. If you find this subject interesting and fascinating, I urge you to do some research at a public library, university library, and/or online. It is my belief that one of the most important factors in the success of future video games is the quality of the story. For that reason, I included this chapter to provide you with an introduction to storytelling itself and techniques that you can use to convey your story when designing your short animated movie or video game.

To learn more about storytelling, visit the following websites:

- National Storytelling Network at www.storynet.org/index.html.

- Aaron Shephard's Storytelling Page at www.aaronshep.com/storytelling/index.html.

- Writing short stories at www.wikihow.com/Write-a-Short-Story

- Writing a play at www.wikihow.com/Write-a-Play

Storytelling in the video game industry is a rather new phenomenon. Most of the video games from the past and some even today do not incorporate a story. However, there are many games that have incorporated a story in simple as well as complex ways. For example, *Pac-Man* and *Donkey Kong* are older games that were successful and incorporated simple stories. *Pac-Man* had intermissions between significant stages. There is an intermission where a ghost is chasing *Pac-Man* and he is getting very close and then the shroud of the ghost is caught on a nail. This stops the ghost's pursuit. This is a simple story, but it adds some entertainment for the players and reinforces the idea of the ghosts chasing Pac-Man. *Donkey Kong* is the game where the character Mario is introduced. Mario is the plumber in the story where the large ape, *Donkey Kong* took a young woman hostage. Mario is the hero who is going to climb all of the construction girders of a building to try to rescue her. This story is simple, but it drives the game forward and makes the game interesting and compelling. It also provides a personality and introduction for the Mario character who has become the focus of several highly successful video games. It is my belief that even in this simple games by today's standards that the stories enhanced these games and increased their entertainment value.

Today's games include much more detailed stories that may be told over a series of games. For example, consider the following excerpt from the Bungie Studios website:

> *(Official Backstory for Halo) (2160-2200) This period in human history was marked by a series of brutal conflicts between various governments and factions in our Solar System. Conflicts of particular historical importance included the Jovian Moons Campaign, The Rain Forest Wars, and a series of clashes on Mars.*
>
> *As overpopulation and political unrest on Earth increased, a number of new political movements formed. The most noteworthy dissident movements of the period were the "Koslovics" and the "Frieden" movement. The Koslovics—supporters of neo-Communist hardliner Vladimir Koslov—sought a return to the glory days of Communism and the elimination of corporate and capitalist influence, particularly in orbital facilities and offworld colonies.*
>
> *The Frieden movement was a resurgence of fascism, springing from anti-Koslovic sentiment that had taken root in the Jovian colonies (largely backed by Unified German Republic corporations, frequent targets of Koslovic "workers' crusades"). "Frieden" literally means "peace." In this case, they believed that peace could be achieved only once the "oppressors on Terra Firma" were eliminated.*
>
> —*Courtesy of http://halostory.bungie.org/halostory.timeline.html*

There is much more to the story and it is composed to a timeline. Each release of *Halo: Halo, Halo 2, and Halo 3* have advanced the story to maintain the interest of the users. I have even heard my own students discuss the anticipation of *Halo 3* because they wanted to see where the story was going and where it would take them next. This story technique is only in its infantile stages, but as the competition for games continues to grow there will be a challenge for game makers to separate their games from their competitors in the gaming markets and the entertainment industry in general. The power of a good story is one of the primary ways this will take place.

During the design process, the story is what you use to organize your thoughts and to provide a guide to developing a movie or a game. Also the story is what engages someone when they play the game or watch the movie. This may seem very obvious for developing a movie. After all, this is what we think of movies as being and in some cases the movie is based on a book or a true story. However, this is not what you would have thought about when developing a game. In this chapter, you will learn about complete design processes and storytelling techniques so that you can begin your own project.

The Design Process

The design process is a very creative type of process. It is important that you follow this process to ensure that you complete the project that you were trying to complete. The design process is designed in a way to keep from having to redo the work you have done before. So what is a design process? It is similar to a set of instructions that you follow when you are creating something.

The following is a design process for developing games and movies that will help to organize your efforts and make your projects more enjoyable and less frustrating. The design process is composed of the following steps:

1. Brainstorm and create an idea.

2. Develop a story.

3. Prototype the story with storyboards.

4. Implement your idea with software.

5. Test your movie or game.

The idea is that you follow these steps and that will help you focus on one aspect of the project at a time and help you be more efficient and successful. What do these steps mean? You will learn more about the details of these steps in the sections that follow. First, I want to revisit a creative process that you have been exposed to in school to give you some insight into what a creative process is like. Then you can dive into the details of the five-step design process for games and movies.

The creative process that I am thinking about is the "writing process" you probably learned when writing an essay or research paper. This is a process that you were taught in school and are expected to use every time you have to write an essay or research paper.

First you develop your idea. During this part of the process you determine what your writing will focus on. For example, you may decide to write an essay on the economic plan for President Barack Obama. Now that you have the topic, you have to find the books, newspaper articles, magazine articles, and other documents that can help you understand his economic plan.

Next you develop an objective or thesis statement for your paper that will be the focus for your paper. This will lead you to develop an outline of your paper. The outline is used for the next phase, which is where you write a rough draft of your paper. After the rough draft is completed, you perform some editing of your paper to make it into a final draft. Now you are ready to do the final proofreading of your paper and finally you submit the paper to your teacher for grading.

Notice that in the writing process there are several stages or phases, and you do not proceed to the next phase until you have completed the previous phase. For example, you do not start writing the rough draft before you have completed the outline. Why is this? The answer is that if you were to start writing the rough draft without an outline you will write a confusing paper. The information could be in the wrong order, or you may not provide enough information, or some other problem will occur. The outline serves as your guide in writing the rough draft and so it must be completed first. The second thing to notice about the process is that each stage of the process is focused on a small number of tasks. A successful process breaks up the work of the entire project, which can be overwhelming, into manageable stages that are less overwhelming.

Third, the process will prevent unnecessary rewriting and rethinking by forcing you to develop your ideas as you move forward. Now it's time to learn about the design process you will use for creating your projects in this book.

In the next few sections, you will dive into the details of the five-step design process that was presented earlier. Keep in mind that it's a creative process and so, just like the writing process, it will require you to repeat steps sometimes. Before going to the next section, let's revisit the five-step process:

1. Brainstorm and create an idea.

2. Develop a story.

3. Prototype the story with storyboards.

4. Implement your idea with software.

5. Test your movie or game.

The next section will discuss Step 1, followed by a section on Step 2, and so on.

Step 1: Brainstorming and Creating an Idea

Brainstorming is where you define your idea and can begin to develop a story. This is where you define things like the audience that you want to target with your project. Is this an idea that would appeal to young children or older kids? Will your game idea appeal to male or females? The audience is important because as you develop your story you want to make sure the story is appropriate for the audience. In addition to the audience, you should think about the theme of your idea. If your idea is a movie, the theme is the message that you want to deliver to the person watching it. What is the idea that your movie will leave with the person? If your idea is a game, you should think about the main objective of your idea. What is the one main objective that the player should have in mind when playing your game? What are the different challenges you want the player to master?

Sometimes, this step can be difficult. Typically the reason is that you do not have enough experience with similar ideas. Therefore, you should do some research on movies or games that are similar to yours. This means you should read about other movies or games, or watch the movies or play the games. As you do this, think about the questions that were just given to you, and see if your idea becomes clearer.

Exercise: Creating Your Idea

Start brainstorming about an idea for an animated movie or game. Get a handful of index cards or divide paper into index-card sized areas. On each index card, label it with Title and Theme/Objective, as shown in Figure 2.1.

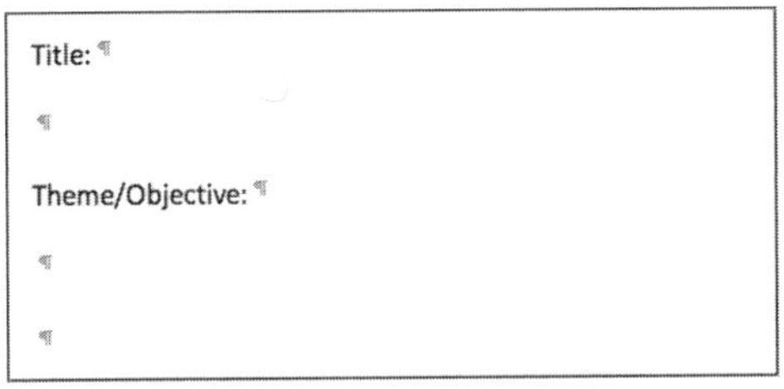

Figure 2.1
Index card with labels suitable for brainstorming.

Each card should cover only one theme/objective. Try to keep all of your information on a single side of the index card. After you have completed an index card with a good idea on it, you can go to the next step.

Step 2: Developing a Story

Developing a storyline for an animated movie or computer game can be a very complex task. Storytelling is a discipline in itself that incorporates several skills and concepts that will not be covered in this book. The goal of this section is to provide you with some basics of storytelling that can help you develop a story that is suitable for your animated movie or game.

Although storytelling isn't always the strongest component of games today, it is playing a more important role. There are not a lot of great examples to choose from, and so you will need to have some confidence and do the best that you can with the story development because it will pay off in the end. On the other hand, if you are developing an animated movie, you have tons of examples of great stories in film, books, and plays. Take advantage of these resources when crafting your story. You may even want to start by choosing one of your favorite stories and then build your movie as an adaptation of that story.

There are several elements that you should include in your story (from Kevin Oxland, *Gameplay and Design*):

- The setting
- The structure
- The story theme
- Character definition
- Emotion
- The dialogue

The *setting* is a collection of ideas that describe when and where the story takes place. Both games and movies have settings. You can use ideas such as dates, historical events, places around the world, or fantasy locations to explain the setting. You should begin your story with an explanation of the setting in a visual, textual, or combined visual and textual way. Remember that if you choose a "real" setting, you must do proper research to ensure that the other elements of the story are also compatible with that setting.

The *structure* of the story is its organization. In movies and plays, the story is divided into acts and scenes. In games, you may have parts and levels or stages. The important part of structure is that you need to have a beginning, middle, and an end. In movies, there are typically three acts:

- The first act introduces the audience to the major characters, setting, and theme. The first act is also responsible for getting the audience's attention.

- The second act is where the main character is taken through a series of events and challenges that take the audience on an emotional ride. We see the characters grow in several ways, and we get to know and understand them.

- The final act is where the theme or lesson of the story is revealed again within the context of the story told in the second act. This is where the story concludes.

In games, you can have the same structure. The first act is your opening screen with the environment and challenges put forth. The second act is the series of levels or stages that pose the challenges to the players. The trick in games is the conclusion because it can end when the player quits or is killed. Otherwise, it must continue to evolve. This is why I suggest using a structure where each stage or set of stages has some conclusion that ties into the theme. For example, in *Donkey Kong* act one, *Donkey Kong* takes the damsel up the scaffolding of the building and dares Mario to save her. Level one then presents the challenge for Mario to navigate ladders, rolling barrels, and fireballs to make it to the top to save the damsel. This was act two for level one. If successful, Mario makes it to the damsel, but then *Donkey Kong* takes her to the next level in the game. This serves as a mini-conclusion or an act three. The player gets a sense of accomplishing the objective, but the ultimate conclusion is not met. To my knowledge there is never a conclusion or act where Mario saves the damsel, but the mini-conclusions play that role in the story.

The *story's theme* will help make the story compelling to its players. The theme of the story is the big picture for the story. The theme could be heroism, bravery, persistence, being highly skilled, and so on. You pick the theme that you would like your story to have, and what lesson(s) you want to teach through your movie or game.

The *characters* are the central part of the story. The characters in stories are what the player identifies with, just like in a movie or a television show. People enjoy movies because they become emotionally attached to the character at some level or the character's situation. In movies, you will develop the characters to have personalities and emotions through the experiences of the character within the story. The audience understands the character by the decisions made by the character and how the character deals with certain situations. In games, characters have been very shallow. They have only been like tools in a toolbox to be manipulated by the player to achieve an objective. However, if you can give your characters *emotion* during the game as feedback to the player, this can allow the player to see and feel what the character feels during the various stages of the game. You should give thought to how you can provide player feedback about their characters' emotion and feelings during the game, and this will add depth to your characters.

The *dialogue* is obviously important in an animated movie. This is where there are significant differences for developing an animated movie versus a game. The animated movie will need an extensive dialogue in the form of a script. You can think of writing your script as a part of your storyboards seen later in this chapter or something separate where you detail scenes and dialogue. Here is a simple example of a script format:

Scene	**Setting Description**
Dialogue and Actions	
Character 1: "Hello, how are you?"	
Action: Character 1 waves	
Character 2: "I am fine; thanks for asking."	
Action: The characters hug	
Character 2: Do you know how to dance?"	
Character 1: "Yes, I do. Do you want me to teach you?	
Etc.	
Describe how the scene should end.	

This very simple script will have you thinking about the dialogue and the small gestures and actions that should also take place during the dialogue. This level of detail is needed in animated movies, but if you are building a game you can probably get away with adding the dialogue to your storyboards only. I will show you storyboards in the prototyping section.

Step 3: Prototyping Your Idea

A very low-tech and simple way to prototype your project is by the use of storyboards. A *storyboard* is a collection of still images similar to a comic strip. The idea is to take key moments of your game or movie and sketch what the moment would look like. You then add commentary about the dialogue that takes place, the sound effects, background music, and actions. You can then put these images into the sequence of the game or movie. This provides a great way to determine if your idea is being conveyed the way you would like it be conveyed. You can share this with your friends and family when it's complete and get their feedback.

This may seem like a very simplistic approach, and you may be thinking that nobody does this. You would be mistaken! Storyboards are used throughout the gaming industry and film industry. Check out these websites:

- Pixar's "How We Do It?" at ww.pixar.com/howwedoit/index.html#. Click on the handle of the viewmaster and you will see that in Steps 1 and 3, storyboards are used.

- Power Production Software at www.storyboardartist.com/successstories. html. Here you will find software used to create storyboards. The software is used by companies such as EA Games:

  "StoryBoard Artist is changing the way storyboarding is done and there's nothing like it on the market that's as fast and easy to use . . . It's opened the doorway to getting storyboards closer to film. Anyone can use it . . . "

  —Ken Harsha, storyboard artist for *Shrek* and *The Simpsons,* Director of Concept for EA Games

- Disney's "The Art of Storyboarding" at filmmakeriq.com/filmmaking-360/ disney-the-art-of-storyboarding.html. Walt Disney has been using story-boards since they first started making cartoons and feature films.

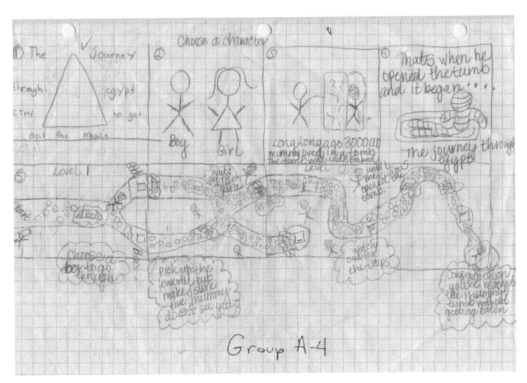

Figure 2.2
Storyboards depicting a story about a journey to Egypt.

You can create your storyboards various ways using various formats. Figures 2.2 and 2.3 show several examples of storyboards created by middle school students.

These storyboards illustrate several ideas. First, notice that they are arranged in order so that they convey the start and end of the story. Secondly, notice that they are sketches. Your storyboards do not need to be polished works of art. I strongly encourage using stick figures if you do not feel that you are a good artist. Third, they both have included dialogue in their storyboards. Finally, note in Figure 2.3 there are examples of directions for camera angles and other actions. In some scenes there are music notes to suggest the inclusion of sounds. These storyboards are representative of the style that you should have in your storyboards.

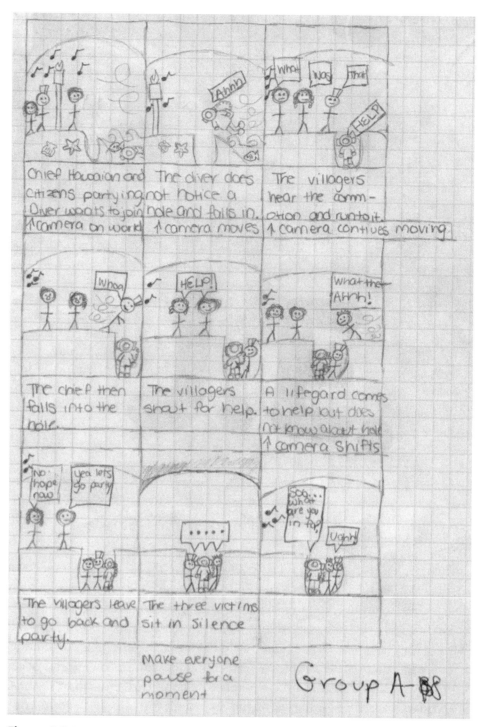

Figure 2.3
Storyboards depicting a story about a Hawaiian king.

In this exercise, you will create a set of storyboards for your story. You should consider the elements of a story, including the setting, structure, theme, character definition, emotion, and dialogue. If you are developing a movie, you should also create a script to go along with your storyboards. In this exercise, focus on creating the storyboards and/or script for one scene or level. Creating storyboards is somewhat of an art, and so there are no hard and fast rules to dictate how much you should put on each storyboard. You should try to find storyboards online and look at them as examples. Then develop your own style that works best for your project. A good rule of thumb that I use is that each storyboard should represent a complete thought or idea within your story. For example, if your story is about what you do to get ready for school, you may have a storyboard that shows each morning activity: brushing your teeth, washing your face, putting on clothes, and eating breakfast. You can use the following template for storyboards or you can develop your own style.

Scene Number:

<<Draw Scene Here>>

Description of Setting:

Sound(s)(background and effects):

Dialogue:

Step 4: Implementing Your Idea

If you have completed the storyboarding phase of the process, you are ready to implement your idea. The majority of the remainder of this book focuses on the implementation of your ideas. However, you deserve to have some background on how implementation can be done.

Implementing your idea means that you will use software programs to create characters and other objects, create your settings and environments, and then program your characters and objects to perform the movie or game you have decided to create. During this process, you may use programs such as Photoshop or Microsoft Paint to create graphics objects that you want to make a part of your movie or game. You can use sound-editing software such as Audacity to create your own sound effects or download sound effects from websites for small fees or free of charge. However, the most important software for you will be the software that allows you to bring it all together and program your project.

In this book, I will introduce you to the Alice programming environment (www.alice.org). The Alice programming environment is a visual programming environment and so it minimizes the need to type tedious commands, and allows you to experiment as you build your project.

The next chapter helps you get started with using Alice and revisits the other software as needed to help you work with images and sounds.

Step 5: Testing Your Game

Testing your project is one of the more interesting challenges. You will always be faced with the problem that your movie or game is not doing exactly what you want it to do. Whenever there is a problem in software that we are writing, we call it a *bug*. *Debugging* is the activity of locating the bugs and fixing them. Finding bugs and figuring out ways to fix them can sometimes be very challenging. My advice to you is to be patient. Do your best to isolate the bug, and always refer to the book for help on correct ways to fix the bug. A *bug* is an error in a process; for example, suppose you were writing instructions on how to bake a cake from the box:

1. Pour cake mix into a large bowl.

2. Add water/milk, eggs, and pudding mix to the large bowl.

3. Pour the batter into the cake-baking dish.

4. Bake for 30 minutes in the oven at 350 degrees.

If you follow these steps, you will identify at least one major problem. There is a step missing that tells you to mix the ingredients. This missing step is called a *bug*. The missing step should be placed between Steps 2 and 3. Without this step, the person following these instructions will not have a cake. However, the process for finding this bug is for the designer (you in this case) to carefully read the steps, and to have others carefully read the steps. The more people that you have reading the steps, the more likely you will find all of the errors in the process.

The same is the case for computer programming. The computer will only follow the steps that you have created. Therefore, if something is not working properly you should read the program very carefully to find the missing or incorrect step(s). Also, you should not be shy about asking someone else to look at it with you. Even if they have never done this before it can help you uncover bugs. The act of explaining your steps to someone else will make you slow down and pay close attention to each step as you explain it. This process will usually help you see problems in your program.

You can also use the computer to help you find the bugs in your projects. To understand this process, consider what you would do to find a hole in a bike tire. One way is to closely examine the tire and perhaps you will notice the tear or hole in the tire. This is the same as reading your steps carefully and looking for mistakes. However, it is possible to use the tire and some water to find the hole. First you fill the tire with air, and then you pour water on a section of the tire and press on the tire. Keep doing this all the way around the tire until you see bubbles! Since you know that the air pushing the water will make bubbles, air bubbles show you where the hole is located. In this same vein, you test your computer programs. Suppose your program is not performing an operation properly. For example:

1. Move the character to door.

2. Open the door.

3. Move the character into the house.

Suppose you see the character move to the door, but then nothing else seems to work. One way to determine the problem is to add commands to the program to tell you what is happening:

1. Move the character to door.

2. Print "I am at the door".

3. Open the door.

4. Print "I am opening the door".

5. Move the character into the house.

6. Print "I am moving through the door".

So after each step, you have what is called an *echo statement* to provide some status information. If your program does not output the statements in Steps 4 and 6, you know there is a problem before you get there. In this case the problem is probably with the *Open the door* statement. What could be the problem? Perhaps the door is locked, and so you should modify your program now:

1. Move the character to door.
   If the door is locked, unlock the door.

2. Open the door.

3. Move the character into the house.

Now the program determines whether the door is locked. If it's locked, the door is unlocked before the character opens the door. If the door is already unlocked, the character can just open the door. The echo statements are statements to let you know the program (or the tire in the analogy) is okay. If an echo statement does not appear as it should, that means you have bubbles coming out of the tire and you have now pinpointed the location in the program where the problem exists.

Finding and fixing bugs can be a lot like detective work. There are some procedures that you can follow to get you started, but occasionally you will have to be creative to find the bugs and to fix them as well. Finding bugs becomes easier with experience. It's like a detective who has solved 100s of crimes; they start to learn criminal tendencies and recognize similarities between cases. Bugs also have tendencies and patterns as well. So the more bugs you have found and fixed successfully, the more likely new bugs will resemble older bugs.

When you complete your own testing and debugging, you should share it with your friends and family. You are allowing them to view or play your project. In the gaming industry, these people are called game testers and the software industry calls them beta testers. The idea is that allowing a small group of people to experience your game or movie will provide you with some feedback on how you can improve it. It's the same premise that is used when you let others read essays and research papers you have written.

Finally, you can get help from other designers. In this book, you will be using software called Alice. The Alice software has a website with a help forum at www.alice.org. I encourage you to become familiar with this website and join the forum (if you're under 18, be sure to get permission from your parents first).

You can ask any question in the forum and you can even upload your projects. There is a wealth of experienced programmers who have been using Alice for years and they are eager to lend their expertise and experience to help you be successful.

Summary

In this chapter, you started your journey of creating an animated movie or game. This chapter started with a presentation of a design process and during this chapter you completed the first three steps of that process. The remainder of the book is focused on the remainder of that process. Keep in mind that I only shared the tip of the iceberg of disciplines such as storytelling, writing scripts, and creating storyboards. If you have deeper aspirations for any of these areas, I suggest that you search online for other resources including websites and books that can help you to master these areas. If you have completed the exercises in this chapter, you should have storyboards and/or a script that details the idea that you have in mind. You are ready to move to the implementation phase, where you can see the fruits of your labor develop as you build it.

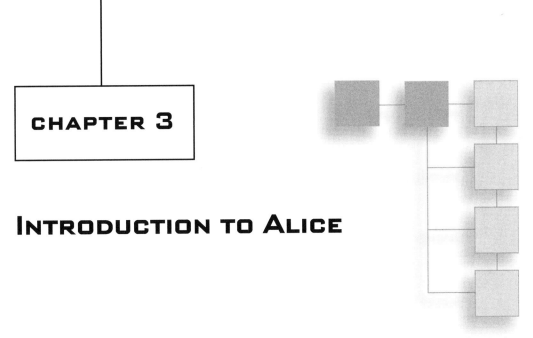

CHAPTER 3

INTRODUCTION TO ALICE

Alice is 3D graphics programming environment that is distributed freely by Carnegie Mellon University (see www.alice.org). Alice is designed to teach beginning and novice students how to program computers by creating virtual worlds for story telling and interactive games. Alice also provides an interactive graphical user interface that allows you to do drag-and-drop programming. The drag-and-drop programming technique simplifies the programming process and eliminates errors that occur when having to type the programs. The result is that programmers can rapidly implement their projects.

Why did I choose Alice for this book? One of the common frustrations for beginning programmers is that if you type the commands of the programming language incorrectly you will get a list of error messages. You must fix these errors before you can see whether the program will execute properly. Alice's drag-and-drop approach enables you to build a program that will always execute. The program may not execute they way you want it to, but it will always do something. This is important feedback for beginning programmers.

Another common frustration for making games and animated movies is the need to create characters and scenery. Fear not, Alice solves this problem as well. Alice is equipped with a large collection of characters and scenery objects that are on your computer and online. The gallery of objects allows you to select objects and immediately start using them. You can even do some customization of the objects if required. Finally, Alice provides a means for publishing your work on the web and is widely used all over the world. Some of the objects found in Alice include:

- **People:** Students, pharaohs, ice skaters, Alice, Cinderella, evil ninja, mad scientists, and so on

- **Animals:** Bunnies, cows, chickens, magic bunnies, hamsters, fishes, cats, snakes, wolves, and so on

- **Beach:** Beach chairs, beach houses, piers, and so on

- **Environments:** Mountains, tree landscapes, grassy landscapes, rooms, and so on

- **Buildings:** Factories, houses, hotels, farmhouses, and so on

- **Nature:** Trees, plants, gardens, ponds, and so on

- **Vehicles:** Cars, airplanes, boats, and so on

This is just a very short list of the objects that you'll find in Alice. There are also objects added periodically through the online gallery.

Can you learn "real" programming using Alice? The answer to this question is yes. Alice has all of the elements of a traditional programming language like C++ or Java. In fact, you can generate Java from Alice programs. Several universities, including CMU, offer introductory programming courses that use Alice. It allows you to explore solutions to traditional programming problems and not just 3D graphics programming problems.

In this chapter, you will learn how to download and install Alice on your personal computer. You may use a Macintosh or Windows PC for installing Alice. Since Alice is free, you may install it on as many computers as you like. You will also learn how to navigate the Alice programming environment, and you will create your first Alice virtual world.

How to Download and Start Alice

Alice is available on the web at www.alice.org, as shown in Figure 3.1. The Alice website is the headquarters for the Alice software. There are several areas that may be useful to you. The teaching area is a good place to go for Alice tutorials, instructional materials, and the newsletter. In addition, under the community

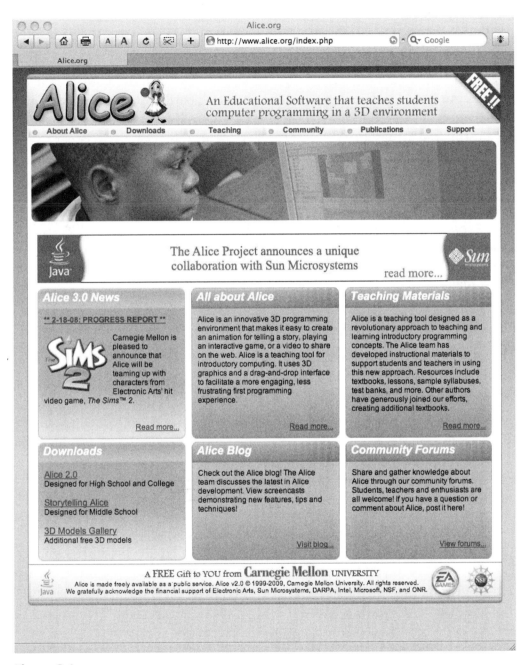

Figure 3.1
Alice's home page, at www.alice.org.

heading there are links to the Alice online community such as the forums, the Alice blog, and the newsletter.

The forums are the best place to go to ask Alice questions or to search for answers. An online forum is an electronic bulletin board. You and others are able to post and answer questions related to using Alice. Alice experts are also monitoring the forum and will provide helpful answers as well. In order to use the forum, you will need to register for free and obtain a login ID and password.

You are ready to download Alice to your computer. Choose the download link on the homepage shown in Figure 3.1. This will bring you to the page shown in Figure 3.2. On this page you have several options depending on the type of computer system you are using. The Windows link will work for Windows XP and Windows Vista. The Mac OS X systems must be at least version 10.3. Any Linux dialect can use the Linux version of the software.

Mac OS X Instructions for Downloading and Starting Alice

The following instructions are for Mac OS X systems. At the completion of these instructions you will be able to start the Alice application, and continue to the "Learning the Alice Environment" section.

1. After clicking the download link, you should see a download window as seen in Figure 3.3. This download window is from the Safari web browser and if you do not see it, you can select Downloads from the Window menu. If you are using another browser such as Firefox or Opera, your window will look different.

2. After the download has completed, a virtual drive will be created and a window will be opened resembling the image in Figure 3.4. If this window does not open, you should look on your desktop for an Alice drive icon or in your Downloads folder for an Alice.dmg file, and then double-click the icon.

3. Drag the Alice icon from this folder to your applications folder. This can be easily done if you open your applications folder in another window, as depicted in Figure 3.5.

4. Double-click the Alice icon to start the Alice application.

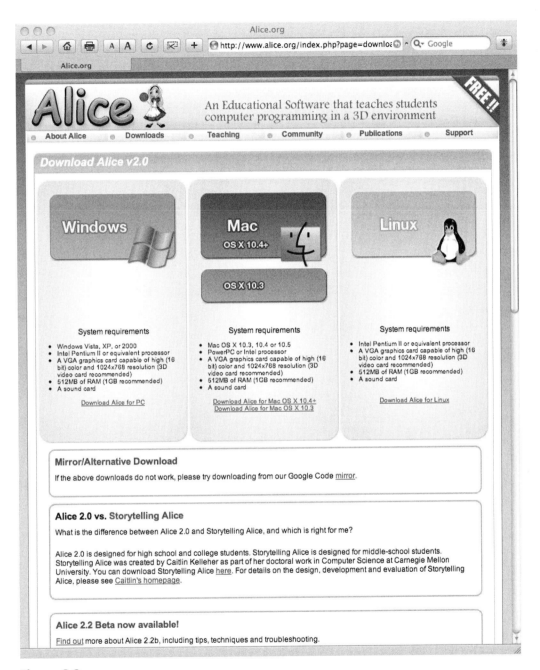

Figure 3.2
The Alice download page for the Windows, Mac, and Linux operating systems.

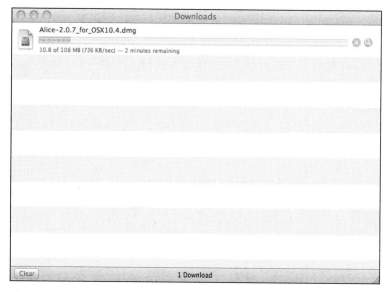

Figure 3.3
Mac OS X Downloads window for the Safari web browser.

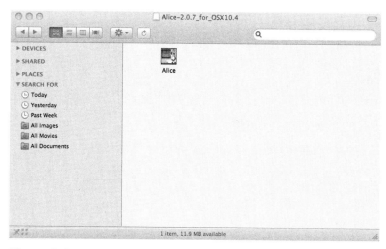

Figure 3.4
Mac OS X virtual drive for Alice with Alice program icon.

Congratulations!! You have successfully installed Alice on your Mac OS X computer system. Now it's time to learn about this exciting new software by proceeding to the "Learning the Alice Environment" section.

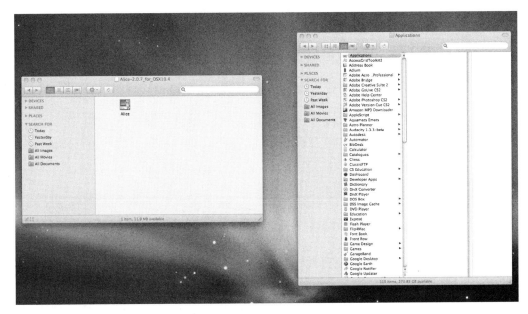

Figure 3.5
Drag the Alice application icon from the virtual drive folder to your Applications folder.

Windows Instructions for Downloading and Starting Alice

The following instructions are for Windows Vista, XP, or 2000 systems. The screenshots are from Windows Vista; and therefore, there will be slight differences from the other Windows systems. At the completion of these instructions you will be able to start the Alice application, and continue to the "Learning the Alice Environment" section.

1. After clicking the download link, you should see the File Download dialog box as seen in Figure 3.6. This download dialog box is from the Internet Explorer web browser. There will slight differences if you are using another browser such as Firefox.

2. Right-click your mouse on the Alice.zip file to open the menu shown in Figure 3.7.

3. Select the Extract All menu item to begin the installation process of Alice.

4. Click the Browse button in the Extract Compressed (Zipped) Folders dialog box to select a destination for the Alice application folder, as shown in

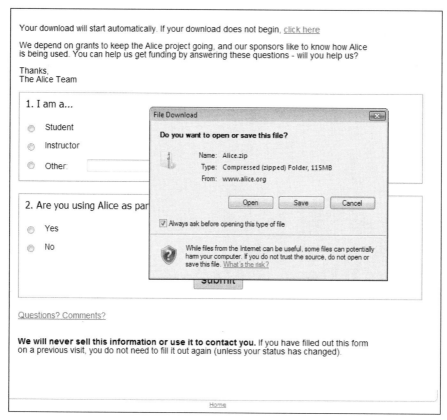

Figure 3.6
The File Download dialog box for Windows Vista Internet Explorer.

Figure 3.8. In this example, the Desktop is chosen, but you may choose your own location. Click the OK button in Select the Destination, followed by the Next button. You will see the progression dialog box in Figure 3.9.

5. Now you will see an Alice folder in your destination folder, as shown in Figure 3.10. If you double-click on this folder, it will unveil a collection of icons. Double-clicking on the Alice icon will start Alice.

Congratulations!! You have successfully installed Alice on your Windows computer system. Now it's time to learn about this exciting new software by proceeding to the "Learning the Alice Environment" section.

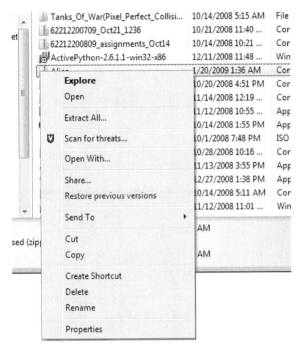

Figure 3.7
The pop-up menu for the Alice.zip file that was downloaded.

Learning the Alice Environment

You start Alice by double-clicking the Alice icon. The Welcome window will be the first screen to appear. It's a multi-tab dialog box. The tabs on the dialog box are labeled as follows:

- **Tutorial:** A collection of built-in tutorials

- **Recent Worlds:** A list of projects there were most recently opened

- **Templates:** The typical starting place for creating a new world

- **Examples:** A collection of working examples that you can open, explore, and modify

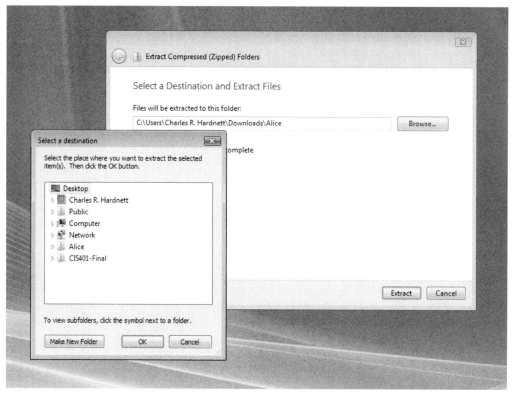

Figure 3.8
The window to select the destination folder for the Alice program.

- **Open a World:** Allows you to use the file browser to find an Alice project on your hard drive or some other storage device

You should start with choosing the Template tab. Select and open the Grass template.

The Alice environment is a single window that is divided into several sub-windows and has two modes:

- **Programming mode:** This is the mode where you can edit and test the programming component of your world. This mode is shown in Figure 3.11.

- **Design mode:** This is the mode where you can add objects to the world and adjust the initial positions of objects in your virtual world. This mode is shown in Figure 3.12.

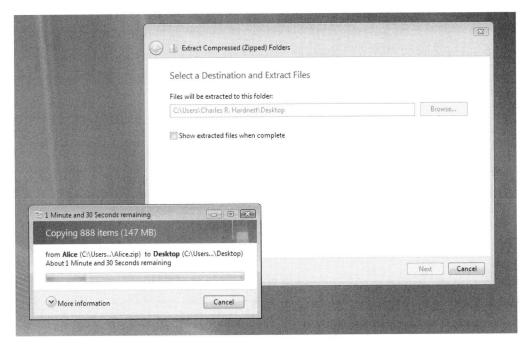

Figure 3.9
The decompression and copying of Alice application files to the desired location.

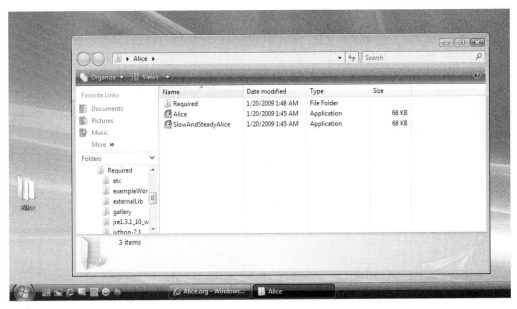

Figure 3.10
The application folder for Alice installed on the desktop.

Currently, you are in the programming mode, and this mode is discussed in the next section.

Programming Mode

Figure 3.11 shows the Alice programming mode. The Programming mode is divided into eight key areas or sub-windows. It's important to have a general understanding of the functionality of each of these areas. But don't worry if you don't understand it all right now. I will remind you of the areas as you proceed through the book. Also, the more you work with Alice, the more familiar you will

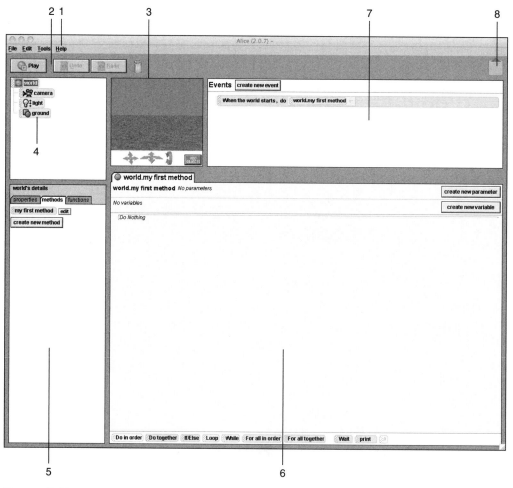

Figure 3.11
Alice's programming mode with areas defined.

become with its environment. Here are the eight key areas of the programming mode, as called out on Figure 3.11:

1. **The Application Menu**: This menu allows you to do some familiar tasks such as open and save files found under the File menu. Click the File menu now and take a look at some of its features. The Edit menu is where you can set preferences for Alice. Click on the Edit menu and then select Preferences, and you will see the preferences that you can use for Alice. The Tools menu is where there are options for dealing with errors in Alice and where you can examine some characteristics of your virtual world that may affect its performance and size. The final menu option is the Help menu. This menu contains online help for using Alice as well as a collection of tutorials for learning some of the basics. I think the tutorials are an excellent way to learn more about Alice.

2. **The Toolbar**: Contains several commonly used functions such as the Play button to start your virtual world, an Undo button for the mistakes we all make, a Redo button to repeat the last action you performed, and a Trash Can for deleting parts of your programs.

3. **The World View Pane**: This window contains the current view of your virtual world. It will expand when you play your world.

4. **The Object Tree Pane**: This is where all of the objects for your virtual world are listed. All virtual worlds have a camera, light source, and a ground at the start. As you add characters and other objects, this tree will grow.

5. **Details Pane**: This area contains details for the currently selected object in the Object Tree. These details include properties that can alter the appearance of the object, and functions and methods that are used to direct the actions of the object.

6. **Editing Pane**: This area is where you edit the program components of your virtual world. These program components are responsible for carrying out the activities of the virtual world.

7. **Events Pane**: This area is where you put program components to respond to various events. An event is something that your world receives at random times and you can decide how to respond. For example, an event could be the user pressing a key to move a character within your world.

8. **Clipboard**: This area is used for copy-and-paste. You can drag program components to the clipboard. Then you can drag information from the clipboard to other areas to paste it.

These are the areas of the Alice programming mode. You will be using this mode throughout the book, and you will be able to practice using these areas on a regular basis.

Design Mode

The design mode is used like a Computer Aided Design (CAD) tool. CAD tools are used to design buildings, bridges, cars, planes, and many other structures and vehicles. In the Alice design mode, you design the scenery and characters for your world. You will place scenery objects into your world and move them around until they are the way you would like them. You will also place your characters into your virtual world as well as create an initial pose for your characters.

To enter the design mode, you click the Add Objects button in the lower-left corner of the *World View Pane* (see Figure 3.11 if you do not remember where it is located). Figure 3.12 shows the design mode window for Alice. The design mode is divided into individual panes in a similar fashion as the programming mode. This discussion is just to give you the lay of the land, and so do not fret if you don't think you can remember all of this now:

1. **The World View Pane**: This is where you can navigate your world during the design mode. You can use the arrows at the bottom to move and rotate your camera to see all parts of your virtual world. You can also drag/move characters around the virtual world using this pane. This is done in the same way you drag objects on your desktop.

2. **Design Mode Controls**: The controls in this area are used to modify the way your mouse controls objects in the World View Pane. The buttons in this pane change your mouse from a dragging control to rotation control, resizing control, or a duplication control.

3. **Camera Controls**: These controls move the camera object to view other parts of the world. The leftmost controls are for panning the camera, the

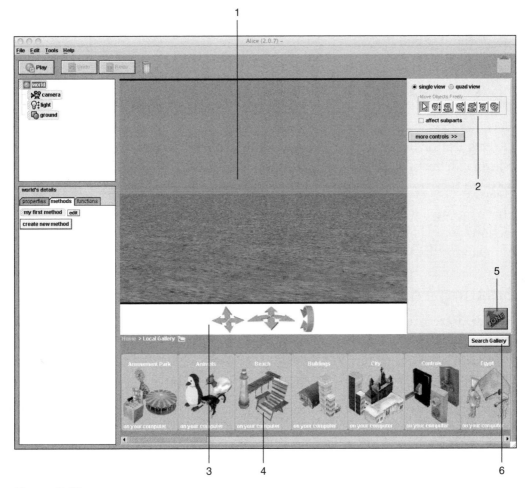

Figure 3.12
This is the design mode of the Alice application window.

middle controls are for zooming and rotating the camera, and the rightmost controls are for tilting the camera.

4. **Object Gallery Pane**: This area is where Alice organizes the objects that you place in your world. The objects are organized into groups such as Animals, People, Environments, and Vehicles, to name a few. There are actually two galleries: a local gallery and an online gallery. The local gallery contains objects installed on your computer and the online gallery contains objects stored on an Alice server.

5. **Done Button**: This button is to switch you from the design mode back to the programming mode.

6. **Search Gallery Button**: This button allows you to perform keyword searches of the local and online object galleries.

Click the Done button to return to the programming mode. Now click the Add Objects button to return to design mode. And of course, clicking the Done button will take you back to programming mode. You will switch back and forth between these two modes on a regular basis.

I have oriented you to the design and programming modes for Alice. In the next section, you will build your first Alice virtual world and have a chance to learn more about the two modes of Alice. Good Luck!

Creating Your First Alice Virtual World

Now you are ready to create your first virtual world using Alice. In computer science we call your first program a "Hello World" program. We are going to create the world together. We will call the world "Bluebird and Bunny". This virtual world will be an animated short story; a very short story. The first step is to develop your storyboards.

There are five storyboards in Figure 3.13. Your storyboards may look something like this when you first start. They depict a very simple story where the Bluebird and the Bunny greet each other. After greeting each other, the Bluebird tells a knock-knock joke. After the joke, they laugh and the story is over. Although this is not a detailed story, it does provide an opportunity to discover various features of Alice, including:

- Creating the opening scene using the design mode

- Creating dialogue between characters using the programming mode

- Moving characters using the programming mode

Like most virtual worlds projects, you will take your storyboards and start working on your scene. In Alice, this means that you will go directly to design mode. In this mode, you can create your scene's environment and add the characters and any other objects. You can even set your characters in opening poses by setting their arms, heads, and legs in the positions that you need to create the appropriate poses. The following steps will get you started with the implementation of this virtual world.

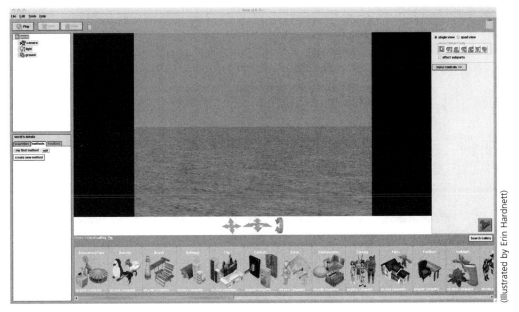

Figure 3.13
This figure shows the storyboards for the "Bluebird and Bunny" short story. These rough sketches show the progression of the short story and will act as a guide in building the world.

Switching to Design Mode

If you are in the programming mode, click the Add Objects button in the World View Pane of the programming mode. This will bring you to a screen similar to Figure 3.12 in the previous section.

1. Find the object gallery pane, and find the Animals folder.

2. Select the Animals folder and look for the Bunny object.

3. Double-click the Bunny object to the World View Pane. If you have done this correctly, it will resemble Figure 3.14. Do not bother the dialog box at this time.

Tip

> The dialog box shown in Figure 3.14 will appear for any object that you add when you double-click on that object in the gallery. It shows various characteristics of the object that is being added. The number of movable parts is an interesting characteristic. It specifies how many parts of the object you, when creating your virtual world, can control. Higher values mean that you will be able to control more parts of the object. The movable parts can be upper-arm, lower-arm, hand, upper-leg, lower-leg, and so on.

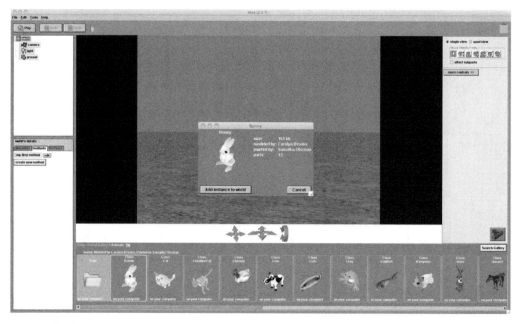

Figure 3.14
This figure shows what happens after you select the bunny and drag it to the World View Pane. The dialog box has some basic characteristics of the bunny object, like the author's name, the size, and number of movable parts.

4. Now you are ready to find the bunny. Click on the Animals folder in the gallery at the bottom of the screen. Once you find the bunny, double-click on the bunny and a dialog box will appear. When the bunny is first added to the world, it is facing to your left (the bunny's right). You need to make your bunny turn and face its left (to the right of the screen). This is accomplished by using the design mode controls found in design mode. In Figure 3.15, these controls are highlighted in the upper-right corner (number 1). You can see where I have selected the third button (number 2). This button allows you to rotate the bunny left and right. Go ahead and select the rotate left and right button from the design mode controls, as shown in Figure 3.15.

5. Select the bunny, and move your mouse to turn the bunny to face the right of the screen.

6. Now it's time to place the bluebird into the scene. To get the bluebird, you will need to switch to the Web Gallery. Select Home in Object Gallery Pane, and then select the Web Gallery.

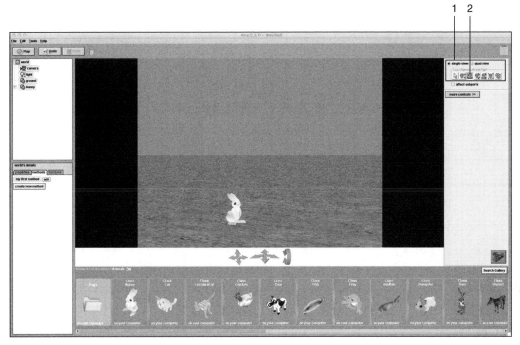

Figure 3.15
This figure shows the result after you have placed the bunny in the scene and rotated the bunny on its y-axis to face the right of the screen instead of the left.

7. Select the Animals folder and locate the Bluebird object.

8. Double-click on the Bluebird object and add it to your world. Figure 3.16 shows the result of this operation.

You should have noticed that the bird is huge compared to the bunny. The bluebird appears to be larger because it is placed closer to the camera than the bunny. In the next section, you will fix this problem by learning to adjust the positions of objects using a four-camera mode called Quad-View.

Using Quad-View to Adjust Objects

The problem exposed in the previous section is that the virtual world is 3D, and objects are made larger to appear to be closer and made smaller to appear to be far away. The problem here is that the bluebird is closer to the camera than the bunny, hence looks like a monster-sized bluebird! To fix this, you need to move the bluebird away from us in the scene and towards the bunny. But it will be hard

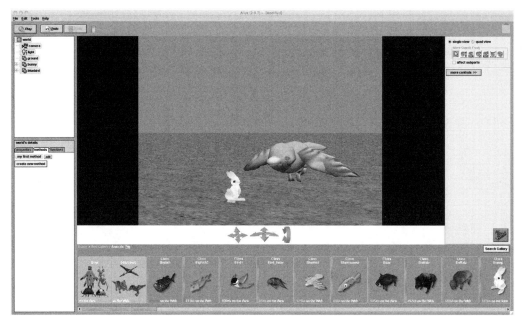

Figure 3.16
This figure shows the result after you have placed the bluebird in the scene.

to determine if the bluebird is next to the bunny unless you have a camera on the side of the bunny or looking down on the bunny. You are in luck! Alice has a feature in design mode called *Quad-View*. Quad-View is where you have four camera angles of your virtual world, as shown in Figure 3.17:

■ The upper-left is the current camera angle

■ The upper-right is a top-view camera angle

■ The lower-left is the right-side camera angle

■ The lower-right is the front camera angle

The current camera angle is based on the camera that you have control of from your object tree. The top-view camera angle is a camera that is looking down onto the world and the characters. So you will see tops of characters' heads in this view. The right-side camera angle is a view based on a camera positioned to the right of the current scene. The front camera angle is based on a camera that is positioned to point at the scene.

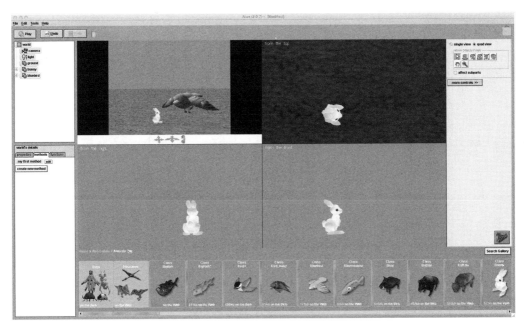

Figure 3.17
This figure shows the Quad-View, which is viewing the scene from four different angles simultaneously.

Now it is time to start making the adjustments to the positions of the characters in the virtual world you are creating. Follow these steps:

1. Select the Quad-View radio button in the upper-right portion of the screen.

2. Click on the bluebird in the World View Pane (upper-left). The bluebird should be highlighted in the object tree.

3. This step will require you to monitor the top-view pane (upper-right) because you are going to move the bluebird back into the scene and you will need to see when the bird is next to the bunny. The top-view will show you when they are next to one another.

   Hold the mouse button down and push the mouse away from you. The bluebird will appear to be moving back into the scene. Continue doing this until the bluebird is next to the bunny in the top-view pane.

4. Select the rotation button you used to rotate the bunny in the previous section (see Figure 3.15, callout 2). Rotate the bluebird to face the bunny. Your scene should now resemble Figure 3.18.

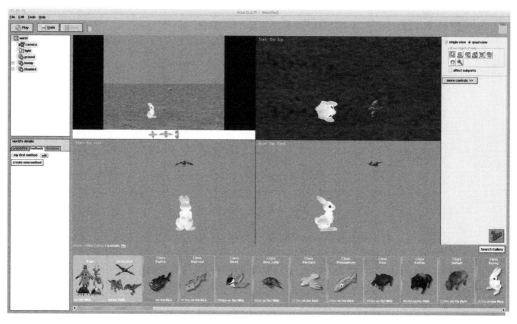

Figure 3.18
This figure shows the result of moving the bluebird to the bunny's left and rotating the bluebird to look at the bunny.

5. Now you need to move the bluebird down because it is currently flying over the bunny. This will be a simple change that uses the design mode controls. Select the arrow from the design mode controls. This will disable the rotation feature.

6. Select the bluebird in the front-view pane (lower-right).

7. Click and drag the bluebird down until your scene resembles the one shown in Figure 3.19.

Now you are ready to program your virtual world, and so you need to go to the programming mode. Do you remember how to do this? If you do remember, go ahead and do it. If you do not remember, click the Done button. Your screen will then look like the one shown in Figure 3.20.

Creating the Dialogue

You should now have a screen like the one shown in Figure 3.20. You will now create a program that emulates the dialogue from the storyboard design. This will include the greetings and the knock-knock joke. To do this, you first need to

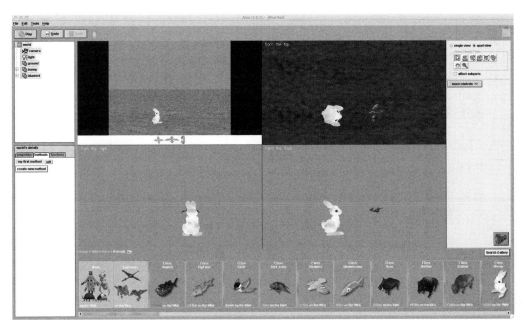

Figure 3.19
This figure shows the result after you moved the bluebird down so that the two characters are eye-to-eye.

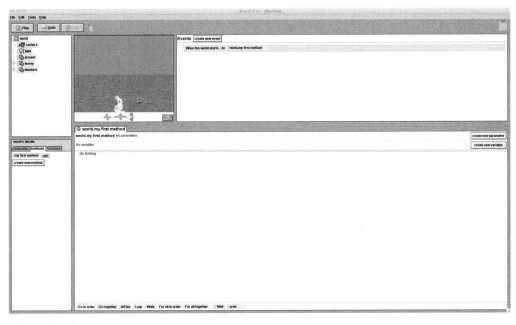

Figure 3.20
This figure shows the completed initial scene within the programming mode.

locate the object tree (See Figure 3.11, callout 4, for a reminder of the object tree location). Now, follow these steps:

1. Select the bunny from the object tree. You should notice that the properties/methods appear in the bunny's details pane (see Figure 3.11, callout 5).

2. Click on the Methods tab in the details pane, and then scroll to find the Say method.

3. Drag and drop the Say method into the Editor pane (see Figure 3.11, callout 6). The result is shown in Figure 3.21.

4. Release the mouse button.

5. From the pop-up menu, you need to select Other and enter the text **Hello Bluebird, I have a knock-knock joke to tell you**.

6. Click OK. You now have your first program instruction from bunny. Congratulations, you are now starting to program a computer!

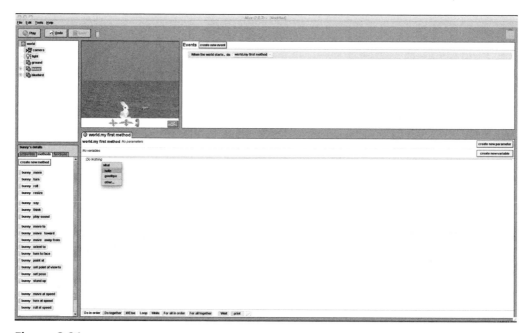

Figure 3.21
The Say command for the bunny is dragged to the programming pane and the pop-up menu appears.

Now let's do that again to make sure you have it. This time you will add dialogue for the bluebird:

1. Select the bluebird from the object tree.

2. Click on the Methods tab in the details pane, and then scroll to find the Say method.

3. Drag and drop the Say method into the Editor pane (see Figure 3.11, callout 6).

4. Release the mouse button.

5. From the pop-up menu, you need to select Other and then enter the text **Okay, go for it!**

6. Click OK again.

Now, you need to finish the dialogue for the story. You will do this by selecting the appropriate character in the object tree and then dragging a Say method to the Program Editor. The order of the dialogue in the Editor will be the order of the dialogue when you execute your world. Make your program look like the one shown in Figure 3.22.

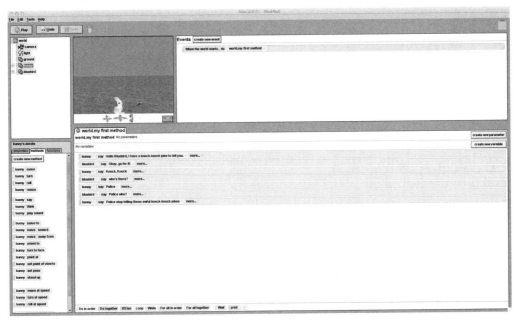

Figure 3.22
This figure shows the result after you have completed the dialogue between the two characters.

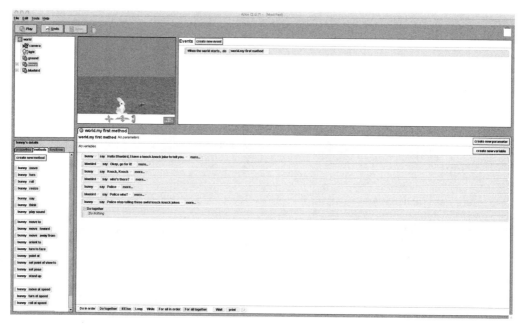

Figure 3.23
This figure shows the placement of the Do Together control-structure.

You need to click on Methods, and then look for the bunny's Say method. You then drag the bunny's Say method to the Program Editor pane, as shown in Figure 3.22.

Once you have finished the dialogue shown in Figure 3.22, it's time to put in the laughter that happens after the joke is told. At this time, you want the bunny and the bluebird to laugh together. If you were to just drag more Say methods, they would laugh in a particular order, but not at the same time.

In Alice, there is a convenient way to express the idea that two actions should occur at the same time. This is called a *Do Together structure*. The Do Together structure tile is located at the bottom of the screen and is colored purple. The following steps show you how to use this powerful structure:

1. Drag and drop the Do Together tile to your editing pane and place it at the end of the dialogue. The result of this step is shown in Figure 3.23.

2. The Do Together tile opens up like it is providing an area for other tiles. You will fill this area with two Say method tiles, one from bunny and one from bluebird. Both Say method tiles will have them laughing as shown in Figure 3.24.

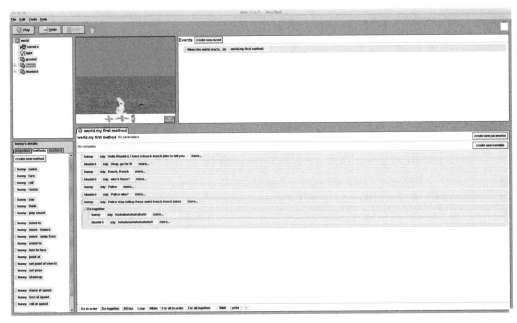

Figure 3.24
This figure shows the complete program with the dialogue and the laughing of the characters.

3. Select the bluebird in the object tree and then drag its Say method to the area provided by the Do Together tile.

4. Repeat Step 3 for the bunny.

Wow! You have just completed your first Alice program. Are you ready to see what it looks like when it's executed? The next section will have you do just that.

Playing Your World

Now that you have completed the implementation of your virtual world, it is time to see the result. Click on the Play button. Your virtual world should play and show a comic strip speaking bubbles containing the dialogue. If there is a problem with your world, stop the playback and go back to the Program Editor.

Exercise: Practicing Virtual World Design

These exercises will give you some more practice with the ideas you learned in this chapter. You should complete some or all of these exercises before moving on to the next chapter:

Change the knock-knock joke between the bunny and bluebird to a knock-knock joke of your choosing. You can find knock-knock jokes at this website: www.knock-knock-joke.com/.

Add another character to the story of the bunny and the bluebird:

1. Create the storyboards for the new story with the three characters, including the new dialogue. Remember you can use stick figures for your storyboards if you would like. The important part here is to determine the dialogue.

   After you have created your storyboards, show them to a friend or family member.

2. Create a new virtual world, place the three characters based on your storyboards, and implement the dialogue from your storyboards.

   After you have created the virtual world, show the same friend or family member how your storyboards match your virtual world.

Summary

Congratulations are in order! You have just created your first Alice program and possibly your first computer program ever. You have learned to take storyboards and convert them to a working virtual world. Also, you have learned how to control the computer and make it perform something that it did not know how to perform before you wrote your program. In the next chapter, you will learn more details about setting up your world in the design mode and how to use the various controls and views found there.

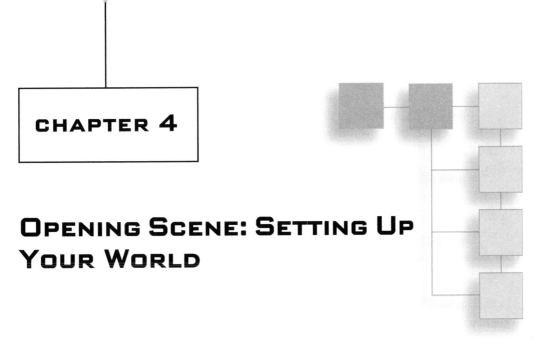

CHAPTER 4

OPENING SCENE: SETTING UP YOUR WORLD

In the previous chapter, you took a virtual world from concept and design to implementation. You started with a set of storyboards and followed those to implement the virtual world. In this chapter, you will dive deeper into the design mode of Alice. One of the purposes of this chapter is to provide you with an understanding of the tools available to you in the design mode. Another purpose of this chapter is to present the common techniques that seem to consistently be required in the design mode. This chapter will cover the following topics:

- The basic principles of 3D graphics

- How to create your setting or environment for your scene

- How to add objects to the environment and place them precisely

- How to manipulate your objects using the design controls and Quad-View

- How to use the camera controls to get the perfect opening camera shot

If you have trouble with any of the exercises, you can simply look at the Chapter 4 folder on the accompanying CD. The folder contains all of the completed examples.

Introduction to 3D Graphics Concepts

Before going into the details for working with objects in the design view, you need to learn a bit about some 3D graphics concepts. First, you should know the difference between 2D and 3D. The term 2D is short for two-dimensional and 3D is short for three-dimensional.

Figure 4.1 shows the difference between 2D and 3D. The 2D space shown in Figure 4.1 (A) has two axes, labeled x-dimension and y-dimension, and so it takes an x-value and a y-value to position an object in the 2D space. You may remember from math class that the x and y coordinates are written with parentheses: (x, y).

Examples of 2D representations are photographs, images on your computer screen, and a drawing on a sheet of paper. In 3D, there is an extra dimension that provides depth. In Figure 4.1 (B) there are three axes, and they are labeled x-dimension, y-dimension, and z-dimension; and so it takes an x-value, y-value, and z-value to position an object in the 3D space. In 3D space, you can identify a point with three values written inside parentheses: (x, y, z). Examples of 3D representations are the world we live in and all of the objects in Alice.

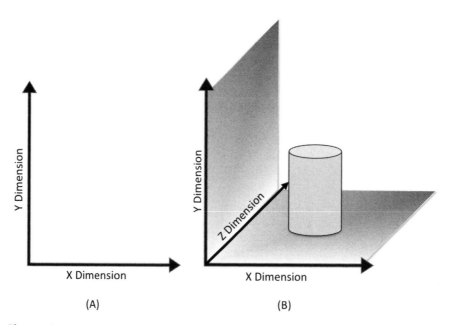

Figure 4.1
This figure shows the two-dimensional coordinate system (A) and the three-dimensional coordinate system (B).

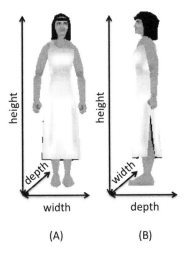

Figure 4.2
This figure shows an object and its dimensions of height, width, and depth.

Objects in 3D spaces are measured in three dimensions also. In Alice, these measured dimensions are called height, width, and depth. In Figure 4.2 (A), the Cleopatra character is shown facing front, with the height, width, and depth labeled. You should keep in mind that these measurements are of the object and do not change because of the orientation of the character. In Figure 4.2 (B), the Cleopatra character has been rotated, but the height, width, and depth continue to measure the same parts of the character.

The next concept has to do with *rotation*. An object in an Alice world can rotate around any of the three axes. Figure 4.3 shows examples of these rotations for each axis. Figure 4.3 (A) is an example of rotating an object around the x-axis. Because the x-axis runs horizontally from left to right, the penguin will rotate towards you or away from you. In Alice, you specify these partial rotations as fractions of a revolution. In each row of Figure 4.3, there is an original position of the object followed by a quarter revolution, a half revolution, and a three-fourths revolution (going from left to right). Figure 4.3 (B) shows the penguin rotating on the y-axis, and this makes the penguin appear to spin like a top. Finally, Figure 4.3 (C) shows the penguin rotating around the z-axis, and this makes the penguin rotate to the left or right (like the propeller on an airplane).

Now you have a general understanding of the basic terminology and concepts of 3D graphics. This will help with understanding some of the issues related to setting up scenes and manipulating objects in the design mode.

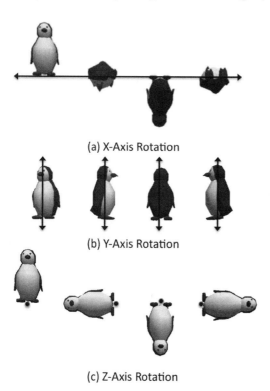

(a) X-Axis Rotation

(b) Y-Axis Rotation

(c) Z-Axis Rotation

Figure 4.3
This figure shows the penguin object rotating on all three axes: x-axis (left-right horizontal axis), y-axis (vertical axis), and z-axis (front-back horizontal axis).

Creating Your Opening Scene

The opening scene is initial placement of characters and objects for your world. The opening scene is typically created in design mode, although you could use the programming mode or a combination of the two. In this section, you will use the design mode because it is the easiest and most natural way to set up your opening scenes. (Recall from Chapter 3 that you can access design mode by clicking the green Add Objects button.)

In this section you are going to explore the controls involved with adding objects to a scene and learn how to move them within the scene to make the best scenes you can.

The scene shown in Figure 4.4 is the goal. To get there, you need to first create a new world. Choose New World from the File menu. The Snow world is where to start. After this, you need to go to design mode by clicking the Add Objects

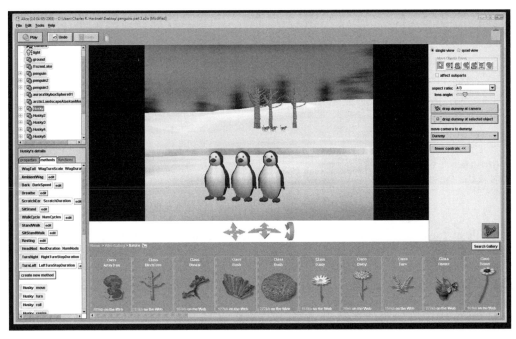

Figure 4.4
This figure shows the opening scene you are going to design in this section.

button. In the design mode, you will actually create the scene. The following steps will not only create the opening scene, but also teach you how to manipulate objects in the scene.

Step 1: Adding a Background Pond

You need to have a frozen lake or pond for the penguins to play on. You will add this first because you want to sit the penguins on it and because it is the center of the opening scene. You will need to go to the Environments folder of the gallery and find the Frozen Lake. The camera will be set to look directly at the lake.

Step 2: Adding the Penguins

You need penguins! To add the penguins, you will need to go to the Local Gallery and select the Animals folder. Select the Penguin and add it to your world. Oops!! She is in the pond, but her feet are not showing. You need to move her up. To do this, you will need to go to the object manipulation toolbox, currently labeled Move Objects Freely, as shown in Figure 4.5.

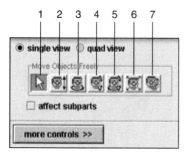

Figure 4.5
This is the Design Mode Controls toolbox.

The Design Mode Controls toolbox has many options for moving objects on the screen denoted by the icons, which are marked on Figure 4.5:

- **Move Objects Freely [1]:** This tool is for free movement of the object. You select the icon and then you can click and drag any object in any direction. This is very useful for general movement, but can be difficult to use when you need to fine-tune the movement.

- **Move Objects Up and Down [2]:** This tool is for moving objects up and down only. You select this icon and then click-and-drag the character and move your mouse up and down until it's in the position you want. The nice feature of this button is that no matter how you move the mouse, the object will only move up and down on its y-axis. This is very useful; especially given the situation here, and so let's use it.

- **Move Objects Left and Right [3]:** This tool is for turning objects left and right. You select the icon and then select your character. You can move your mouse left and right to make the character turn to its left and right. This button is used when you want to change where your character is looking, because it will only turn around the y-axis, as if the character is spinning around on a pole.

- **Move Objects Forward and Backward [4]:** This tool is for turning objects forward and backward. You select the icon and then select your character. You can move your mouse up and down to make the character turn backward and forward, respectively. This button can be used to make your character appear to be falling forward or backward. The character will only turn on the x-axis, as if it's spinning on a rotisserie.

- **Tumble Objects [5]:** This tool is for turning objects in any direction. You select the icon and then select your character. It works just like the other turning buttons, but this time you can rotate the character in any direction. You can make your character rotate on its x-, y-, or z-axis.

- **Resize Objects [6]:** This tool is for changing the size of the character. You select the icon and then you select your character. Moving the mouse away from the character increases its size, whereas moving towards it decreases its size.

- **Copy Objects [7]:** This tool is for making copies of your objects. You select the icon and then every time you select an object, it will duplicate that object. You have to be careful with this tool because everything in the scene is an object and clicking anywhere in the scene will create a duplicate object. Always look at your object tree to see the changes if you do not see them in the camera view.

Click the Move Objects Up and Down button (number 2 in Figure 4.5) and then click the penguin and drag her up until you see her little feet.

You now need to create two more penguins. Use the Copy Objects tool to make these copies. First click the tool icon, and then click the penguin twice. If you have done all of that properly, you should have something like what is shown in Figure 4.6.

Step 3: Arranging the Penguins

Now it's time to put the penguins in a single line side-by-side as shown in Figure 4.7. To line up the penguins precisely, you need to be able to see the line of penguins from the top and from the side as well as the front. These three angles will allow you to get all of the necessary perspectives to verify that the penguins form a straight line.

Select the Quad-View. You will notice that you don't see all three penguins in all three views. You need to get all three penguins in all four views, and you will you use the Scroll View tool from the toolbox shown in Figure 4.8.

- [1] shows the Scroll View tool. You select this icon and your mouse pointer will change to a small hand. You can now use this tool in any of the views. You simply click-and-drag the hand and you will see the view scroll in that direction.

Figure 4.6
This figure shows the design at the point that the pond and three penguins are placed into the scene.

Figure 4.7
This figure shows what happens after the penguins have been lined up side-by-side, shoulder-to-shoulder.

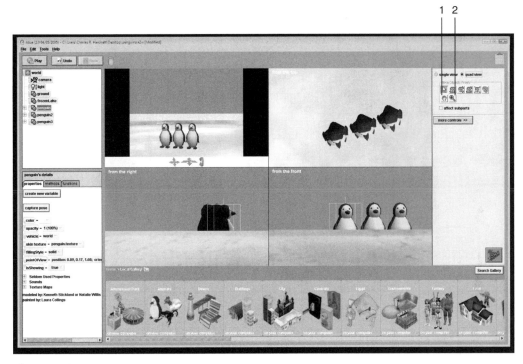

Figure 4.8
This figure shows the Quad-View of the design mode.

- [2] shows the Zoom View In and Out tool. You select this icon and then move your mouse to the view you want to zoom in or out within. Click-and-drag the mouse up to zoom in and down to zoom out.

Step 4: Adding the Sky

Now that you have the main characters in place, you can start to add the backdrop. In the Environments folder, find the folder called Skies. These objects are designed to add more personality to your scene by providing different textures for the sky and horizon. You are going to use two of these skies: one for the trees and nighttime feel and the other for the snowy hills.

Select the Environments folder from the local gallery. Then select the Skies folder. You are looking for the Aurora Skyline object. This object will change the sky and provide the tree line that you see in Figure 4.9.

Step 5: Adding the Hills

Now, it's time to add the hills to the landscape. To do this, you need to select the Arctic Landscape Alaskan Mountains and add it to your virtual world. Voila!!

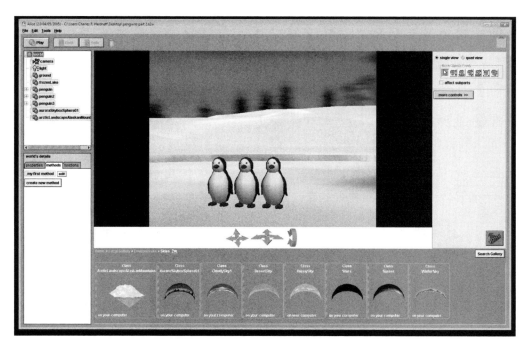

Figure 4.9
This figure shows the result of Steps 4 and 5, which added the sky texture, tree line, and hilly landscape.

This adds some very nice character and depth to your world. You may need to adjust the position of your penguins because the floor of the Arctic landscape will lie over their feet. You should use the Move Objects Up and Down tool from the object manipulation toolbox to make these adjustments.

Step 6: Adding the Background Characters

Now you want to add the background characters that are in the hills, as shown in Figure 4.10. To add these characters, you'll many of the same tools you've already seen. I will also show you a few new techniques that will be useful for your future designs.

First, you will add the pack of huskies in the back. This can be done the hard way or the easy way. Raise your hand if you want the easy way . . . I thought so. In computer programming, the "easy" way is also considered the efficient way. The pack of huskies is composed of five huskies.

Caution

I must warn you that I am going to use the Web Gallery for some of these objects. If you do not have an Internet connection or your connection is very slow, just use substitutes from the Local Gallery.

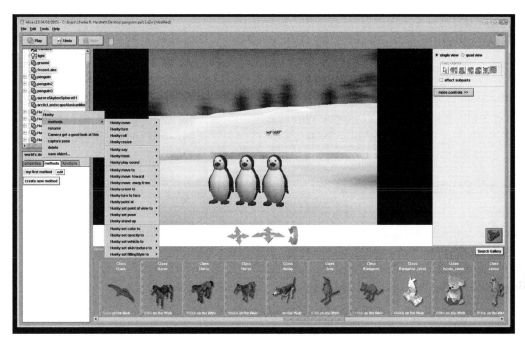

Figure 4.10
This figure shows the pop-up menu for the selected object in the object tree.

Select the Web Gallery and then find the Animals folder. Select the husky and add it to the world. Now, when I did this, the husky was placed behind the penguins. This makes it hard to select.

Tip

Use the object tree to select the husky instead of trying to move the mouse pointer onto the husky in the scene:

1. Select the husky in the object tree.

2. Right-click and a pop-up menu will appear, as shown in Figure 4.10.

3. Move the mouse to the Methods menu, and then the Husky Move menu, and then the Up menu, and finally select 1 meter (1 meter is approximately 1 yard). The menus open as you move the mouse.

Now the husky has been moved up 1 meter into the air. This makes it visible, and it can be easily selected using your mouse at this point.

If you use the tip in this section, you can move the husky above the penguins to make it easer to select. Now, click the Move Objects Freely tool in the toolbox.

Now use your mouse and click and drag the "flying" husky. You will be pushing the mouse to make the husky appear to be moving back to the hilly landscape.

Step 7: Creating a Husky Pack

To get the pack of huskies, you need to make sure the husky is still selected. Now select the Copy Objects tool from the toolbox. Each time you select a husky, another one will be created. If you click the husky four times, you'll have a pack of five huskies.

Step 8: Adding Trees

Now go to the Web Gallery and find the Nature folder. Find the Birch Tree and add four trees using the Copy Objects tool. Next, you will move the trees to where the huskies are located. See Figure 4.11.

Step 9: Moving the Trees

To move the trees to the huskies, you can use some of the methods built into all Alice objects. The methods are actions that the Alice objects can perform. There is a method that tells an object to move to the same location as another object.

Figure 4.11
This figure shows the pop-up menu from an object in the object tree. Here, you are selecting the Birch Tree object.

Select Birch Tree in the object tree. It does not matter which one you select for this exercise. Right-click on the name in the object tree, and you will see a pop-up menu. In Figure 4.11, this menu is shown after you have selected Methods in the first menu and then Birch Tree Move To from its submenu. Now you should select one of the huskies as the target object. The tree will now slide back to where the huskies are. Repeat this for each birch tree and choose different target huskies just for fun. If you make a mistake, you can always press the Undo button at the top of the screen. You can even press the Undo button more than once to undo multiple changes.

Step 10: Using Dummy Drop to Save a Scene

Now you have a scene where the birch trees and the huskies are together in the background. However, because you moved the birch trees to the location of the huskies, the trees and huskies are now on top of one another. You need to fix this, but the camera is too far away to see that level of detail. So you need to move the camera, but you also want to save this camera position so you can come back to it. This introduces the concept of *dummy drop* in Alice, which allows you to save the positions in the virtual world that you would like to use later. You can save positions based on the camera or an object in the world.

On the right side of the screen you have the toolbox and below it is a button labeled More Controls. Select this button to reveal a collection of new controls. These controls are shown in Figure 4.12.

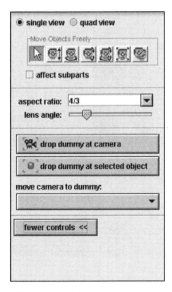

Figure 4.12
This figure shows the additional controls revealed by the More Controls button.

Click the button that is labeled Drop Dummy at Camera. This will drop a marker at the current camera position. The only noticeable change will be in the object tree. At the bottom of the object tree there will be a new folder called Dummy Objects and inside is an object called Dummy.

Let's change the dummy object's name to Start Position. To do this, right-click on the name Dummy in the object tree and select Rename. Now you can type **Start Position**.

Step 11: Adjusting the View

Now you need to move the camera to get a closer look at the birch trees and huskies. The birch trees and huskies are on top of one another. You need to fix this, but to do that you need to zoom into the birch trees and huskies.

Right-click on the Birch Tree object in the object tree, and select Camera Get a Good Look at This. Doing so will move the camera so that your view will be looking down on the trees and the huskies.

Now you can use your toolbox and mouse to move the trees and huskies so that they are similar to the scene in Figure 4.13.

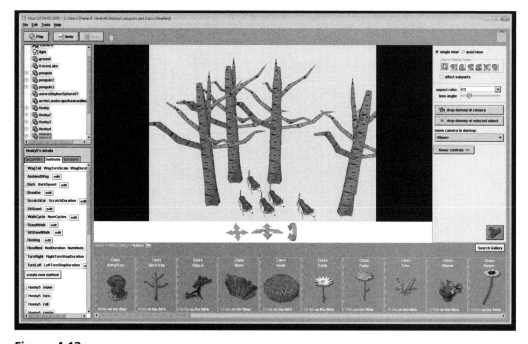

Figure 4.13
This figure shows the result after the camera has been moved to look at the trees and after the trees and huskies are moved away from each other.

Figure 4.14
This figure shows the completed scene for the three penguins.

Step 12: Moving Back to Start

You are almost done. You need to return the camera to its original position. Thankfully, you saved its position as a dummy object that you renamed Start Position.

Right-click on the camera, select Methods from the pop-up menu, and then select Camera Set Point of View To; and then choose Start Position from the final menu. The camera will move back to the start position. You have completed your scene, as shown in Figure 4.14. Congratulations!!!!

Summary

In this chapter, you learned how to create opening scenes. You started by learning about the principles of 3D spaces and worlds. These principles help you to understand the challenges of positioning objects in the world correctly. You also learned about the controls toolbox and how its tools can be used to manipulate characters and scenic objects. You also learned some key features available in Quad-View that give you four cameras to view your world during the scene setup phase. Finally, you learned how to use dummy objects to safely move the camera around your world. These dummy objects help you to get better views of your world and still be able to return to the original camera position. All of the techniques in this chapter are used in other places in this book. Also, you will learn how to manipulate the camera in other ways as well.

In the next chapter, you learn how to add interactivity to your worlds so that you can do things like move a character with the mouse or keyboard. Let's continue the journey!

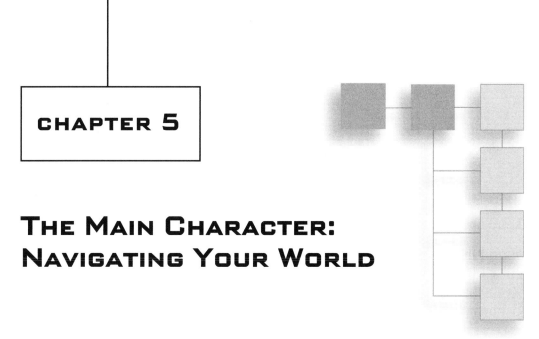

CHAPTER 5

THE MAIN CHARACTER: NAVIGATING YOUR WORLD

One of the common features of the social network virtual worlds and video games is that the players can interact with the worlds through their characters. You can use the mouse, keyboard, gamepad, dance pad, or other input device to control your player in the virtual world of your social network or game. In this chapter, you will learn about the features that Alice provides to add interactivity in your projects. Specifically, the following topics will be covered:

- Introduction to events

- Basic keyboard events

- Navigating with the keyboard

- Navigating with the camera

The examples of this chapter are located on the accompanying CD within the Chapter 5 folder.

You may have noticed that I did not include mouse control in this list of topics. One reason for this is that keyboard events are much more useful in Alice than mouse events when navigating a virtual world in Alice. Also, if you want to use mouse events, you simply follow the same steps as using keyboard events; you just have few options since you don't have as many buttons on a mouse as you have keys on a keyboard.

This chapter is the first of many chapters that will focus on how to program with Alice. This means that you will be learning how to move objects in the virtual world in an automated fashion. You already did this in Chapter 3 when you created the simple world with the bunny and the bluebird. A *program* is a sequence of commands that tell a computer what to do. In the bunny and bluebird example, you told the computer how to make the bluebird and bunny have a conversation. A *programming language* is a set of commands, control structures, and data structures that allows you to program a computer.

A command tells the computer to perform an action such as the command Say in Alice that you used in Chapter 3 to make the bluebird and bunny speak to one another. A control structure allows you to control how groups of instructions are performed; an example is the Do Together structure that tells the computer to execute the commands in the structure at the same time. You used this in Chapter 3 to have both the bluebird and the bunny laugh at the same time. Data structures organize the data in your programs; an example is having a list of objects (an example of this is shown in Chapter 7 for detecting collisions with more than one object in the world). Therefore, Alice is a programming language. It's different from most programming languages because it allows you to program by dragging and dropping instead of typing.

In this chapter, you will be programming Alice to allow you to manipulate your Alice objects and virtual world using the keyboard. For example, you will be able to move a character in Alice around the world using the keyboard when you have completed this chapter.

Let's get started with the first topic that will introduce you to events in Alice. This is going to be a fun chapter!

Introduction to Events

A program *event* is something that happens at some undetermined time. When the event happens, you want your programs to have a way to react to the event. An example of an event in Alice is when the user presses a key on the keyboard or moves the mouse while the virtual world is running. If the users are playing a video game you created in Alice, you cannot predict when they will press a specific key on the keyboard or even whether they will press any key. The unpredictable actions by users is what Alice calls an event. Figure 5.1 shows the Events section of Alice's programming mode.

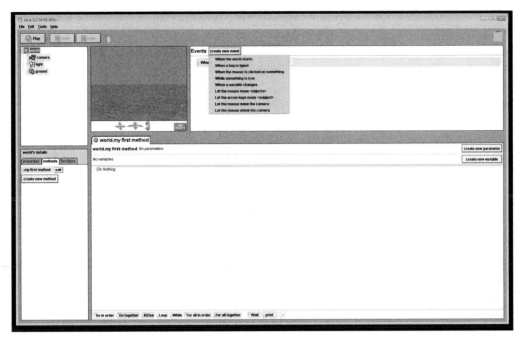

Figure 5.1
The Events section of the programming mode. The Events section is located in the upper-right corner of the programming mode.

There are several types of events that can occur when you're writing programs. Each programming language determines which events it will allow the programmer to handle and how the events are handled. Alice is no different. Alice is a programming environment with its own programming language. The Alice programming language supports events and the following is the list of events supported by Alice:

- When the world starts

- When a key is typed

- When the mouse is clicked on something

- While something is true

- When a variable changes

- To let the keyboard move a subject

- To let the mouse move objects

- To let the mouse move the camera

- To let the mouse orient the camera

Now, I'll give a short definition for each of these events and a short explanation of how you might use each of the events.

When the world starts: This event is activated when the user presses the play button to start the world. This event is used to execute the method that should be used to set the virtual world up in the proper manner. By default, this event is already added and it executes the world.my first method method.

When any key is typed: This event is invoked when the user presses a key on the keyboard. This event has the ability to distinguish between the keys that are pressed. This feature is good for allowing the user to control a character with the keyboard, such as by using the arrow keys.

When the mouse is clicked on something: This event is invoked when any of the mouse buttons are pressed while the mouse is over an Alice object. This event could be useful if you want to use the navigation feature found in many social network virtual worlds whereby the users simply click on the place their avatars should go and then the avatar moves to that area on the screen.

While something is true: This event is activated when the *something* becomes true. The *something* is typically a condition that can be either true or false. For example, suppose you want your game to play as long as your character still has money, but when the users lose all of their money, the game should end. The *something* condition in this case would be money > 0, and when money becomes 0 this would be false and the event would detect that fact.

When a variable changes: This event is activated when a variable in your program changes. A variable is a name in your program that can hold data values. A good use of this event could be in a game where you want to update the players' scores as they earn points. The variable would change when it is updated with a new score because the users earned some points or lost points. When this variable is changed, the event is activated.

Let the mouse move objects: Here, you can replace the word *objects* with the actual object you want to use. In this case, Alice is allowing you to fill in the blank with a single Alice object or a group of Alice objects. This event can be used if you want the mouse to control the movement of your character.

Let the keyboard move subject: In this case, Alice uses the word *subject*, but it is same as an object. This event is used to connect the keyboard to an object or group of objects. This event can be used if you want the keyboard to control the movement of your character.

Let the mouse move the camera: This event is used to give the mouse control of the movement of the camera. The camera is typically in a stationary position or in programmed positions. This feature allows you to build a virtual world, and then allows the users to explore the world using the mouse.

Let the mouse orient the camera: This event is used to give the mouse orientation control of the camera (allowing it to change the tilt and pan of the camera). This feature is also good to use if you want to give your users the ability to explore a given area of your world like a room, but you want them to feel as though they are standing still.

This completes the short introduction to what events are and what types of events are handled in Alice. The use of events can add wonderful experiences for the users of your virtual worlds. You should consider using events in creative ways to make the experience of using your world an exciting experience.

Using the Keyboard Events

The first form of interaction you'll embark on is using the keyboard. The keyboard has been the main input device for computers for decades. Early games utilized the keyboard exclusively because joysticks were not always available with personal computers and they were typically a luxury expense. In addition, the keyboard was always available, and therefore players could always play the game even if they did not own joysticks.

The keyboard is a very flexible input device compared with the joystick. Joysticks typically have only a few buttons and the joystick controls direction and possibly acceleration depending on the game. However, the keyboard has over 100 keys! That means that you have over 100 ways that users can interact with your virtual worlds. You could really go crazy and start introducing key combinations using the Control, Shift, and Alt keys to increase the number of possibilities.

Using the Keyboard for Basic Actions

The first interaction you'll learn is a basic action whereby the pressing of a particular key on the keyboard makes the character perform an action such as

Figure 5.2
This figure shows the two chicken folders in the Web Gallery. Pick the chicken on the left for this example.

jump, make a sound, or flap its wings. With Alice, you can make anything happen due to you pressing a key. You are going to create the event that will allow your users to make the chicken's wings flap by pressing a key on the keyboard.

To get started, you need to create a new world and add a character to your world:

1. Choose the File menu and select New World.

2. Click Add Objects in the World View Pane to go to the Design Mode.

3. Click the Home link in the Object Gallery.

4. Click on the Web Gallery and locate the Animals folder.

    You are about to add a Chicken object to your world. Unfortunately, there are two chickens, and you need to pick the correct one. To help you with that, I have provided the icon in Figure 5.2.

5. Click the chicken icon that resembles the icon on the left in Figure 5.2.

    Now you will create your first event to handle keyboard events. In other words, you are about to program Alice to flap the chicken's wings when the users press the Spacebar on the keyboard.

6. Click the create New Event Button in the Events section and you will see a drop-down menu like the one shown in Figure 5.3. Select the When Any Key Is Typed option from the menu. This will insert an event for when a key is pressed.

7. Let's use the Spacebar as the activating key. Looking at Figure 5.3 again, select the Any Key in red. Then select Space from the menu. This menu will allow you to select any key. At the bottom there is an option for letters and numbers to select their key.

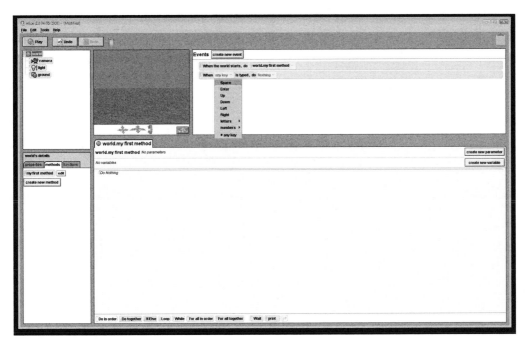

Figure 5.3
This figure shows the new event and the "Any Key" menu item for the event.

8. Select the chicken in the object tree, and then below the object tree select the Methods tab. This will open up a list of methods.

Tip

A *method* is an action that an object can perform. In Alice there are two types of methods: custom and common methods. Common methods are available for all Alice objects; custom methods are only available for a particular type of object. In the Methods tab, there is a list of methods; first you see the custom methods and then you see the Create New Method button. In this case they are flap, peck, and walk. These are custom because not all objects flap and peck. The common methods are next in the list below the Create New Method button. The common methods are move, turn, roll, and many others. These are generic methods that can be used by any object.

The method you are going to use is flap. The flap method requires two values to control the number of flaps and the speed of the flaps. The speed is useful for special effects like slow motion. You would choose smaller values for speed if you want a slow-motion effect.

9. Drag and drop the flap method to the red text labeled "Nothing" next to the When Any Key Is Typed event you just created.

Figure 5.4
This figure shows the submenu that pops up for the values needed by the flap method.

10. A submenu will pop up like the one shown in Figure 5.4. You need to select 1 and then select 0.5. The first value, 1, is used as the "times" argument. The second value, 0.5, is used as the "speed" argument.

If you have completed Step 10 properly, your screen should look like Figure 5.5.

11. Now you can test the new key assignment by clicking the Play button, and then you can press the Spacebar to see the chicken's wings flap. If you hold down the Spacebar, they will only flap once.

Now you have made your world interactive. It's a very simple interaction, but you will build on these concepts to do more. For now, let's explore another feature of the When Any Key Is Typed event. The When event works only as long as you press and release the Spacebar and then press again. However, what if you just want to make the wings flap as long as you hold down the Spacebar? To do this, you can change the When event to a While event. The While event performs the action you assign for as long as the key is pressed.

Figure 5.5
This figure shows the event after it has been assigned a key and a method.

To make this change, do the following:

1. Right-click on the event, as shown in Figure 5.6. Select the Change To option and, from the submenu, select While. This will open more fields, as shown in Figure 5.7. The While has three methods you can manipulate: Begin, During, and End. Begin is where you place a method that you want to execute when the user first presses the Spacebar. During is where you place the method to execute while the Spacebar is still held down. End is for the method that executes when the user releases the Spacebar.

2. Click and drag the flap method to both the Begin and the During parts of the event. Let's assume that when users release the key, they want the wing flapping to stop.

3. Now it's time to see your handy work. Just press the Play button. Then try holding down the Spacebar and see the chicken continue to flap.

This example shows how you can program Alice to have your characters or any object respond to keyboard input. You can use common object methods like Say

Figure 5.6
This figure shows how to change the When event to a While one.

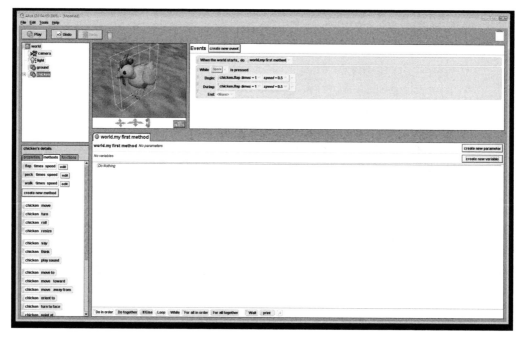

Figure 5.7
This figure shows the While version for key pressing.

and Play Sound to make your keyboard input show cartoon dialogue bubbles or to play sounds, including your own voice! This will be in Chapter 9.

Using the Keyboard to Move a Character in the World

If you have ever played a computer game that moves characters with the keyboard, you know that usually we use the arrow keys or the WASD keys. Alice has provided a convenient way to program the arrow keys to move characters. However, you don't have the flexibility you would have if you used the method from the previous section. I am showing you this method because it's a quick way to get some basic movement, and as you finish your project you will probably want to change it to the more flexible version.

This feature requires just two steps:

1. Click on the Create New Event button as shown in Figure 5.8, and select the Let Arrow Keys Move *subject* option.

2. Click on the Camera reference, as shown in Figure 5.8. The pop-up menu will appear, and you can choose Chicken and then Entire Chicken.

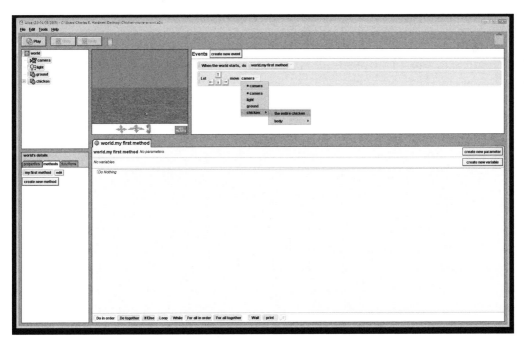

Figure 5.8
This figure shows how to set up the arrow keys to control movement of some event.

If you don't choose the entire chicken, you will split the chicken into parts when you start moving it and it will give you nightmares.

3. Now you can click Play to start the world and then you can use the arrow keys and move the chicken around on the screen.

   Up-arrow moves the chicken forward
   Down-arrow moves the chicken backward
   Left-arrow turns the chicken to its right
   Right-arrow turns the chicken to its left

This method is great for quickly adding the ability to let the users move a character in your virtual world. However, it is limited because you cannot change any of the arrow keys, which may be important to you in advanced projects. If you want to change the behavior, you have to go back to the method presented in "Using the Keyboard for Basic Actions". This is the focus of the next section.

Customized Keyboard Movements for the Character

Now that you have seen how to move characters, it's time to learn how to move characters so that they appear to be walking. You need to accomplish two things in order to do this in Alice:

- You must create an event for each key as either a When or While key is pressed. Most of my students prefer the While version of the key being pressed.

- You will need a method for the character you are controlling that gives the character the ability to walk. Unfortunately, this is not always available in people and animal objects at the moment. I will show you how to determine if it's available in an object, and in the next chapter I will show you how you can create your own walking motion for any character.

Since you have already seen how to do the basics needed to associate an event with a key press, I want to show you how to determine whether a character in the Alice gallery has the ability to walk. Most of the characters in Alice that have the ability to walk by default are stored in the Web Gallery. If you go to the Web Gallery and you select a character such as the cow shown in Figure 5.9, you will see the name of the object, the number of parts, and the methods. In this case, the cow shows that it has a walk method. Therefore, you know that you can move the cow and make the appearance of walking.

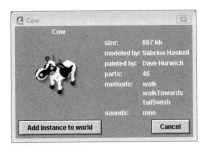

Figure 5.9
This figure shows a walking-enabled character (the cow) and a non-walking-enabled character (the dragon) from the Alice gallery.

However, the dragon shown in Figure 5.9 does not have a method for walking. In this case, you have to look at the number of parts to give you an idea of whether or not you can make it walk. The dragon has 19 parts, including wings, legs, arms, head, neck, body, parts of arms, parts of legs, and so on. This tells you that there is a good chance that you can program the arms and their parts along with legs and their parts to create a walking effect. If the character has very few parts or is only one part, you will not be able to make it appear to be walking.

In this example, I assume you have the first scenario where the character has a walk method. If you do not have a character in your world with a walk method, go back to the section called "Using the Keyboard for Basic Actions" and follow the first five steps to add the chicken character to your world.

Use these steps to get a cow that walks as it moves on the screen:

1. Select the When Any Key Is Typed event from the Create New Event menu. You will need to repeat this step four times to cover the four arrow keys.

2. Right-click on each of the new events, and change the When event to While, as shown in Figure 5.10.

3. Now it's time to assign an arrow key to each event. The result is shown in Figure 5.11. To do this, select the Any Key from the event and then the drop-down menu will show Up, Down, Left, Right, and so on. Select a different key for each event so that you have one event for the Up arrow, one for the Down arrow, one for the Left arrow, and one for the Right arrow.

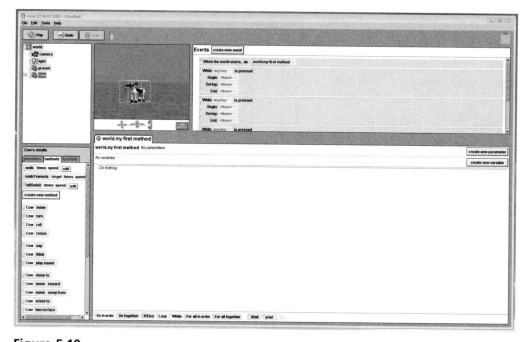

Figure 5.10
There are four events to correspond to the four arrow keys. The events are all changed to be While instead of When.

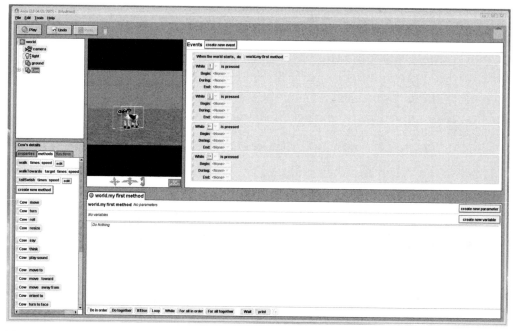

Figure 5.11
Assign one of the four arrow keys to an event.

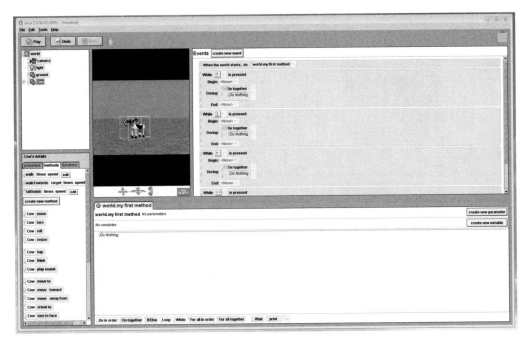

Figure 5.12
The Do Togethers have been added to the events.

Now it's time to place the methods into the events. First, you only need to handle the During phase since that's when you want the cow to appear to be walking. Secondly, the cow needs to move in a direction while its legs are being moved by the walk method. This requires that more than one action be done at a time. Alice has a way of handling these problems. It's called a *Do Together*. A Do Together is a programming statement that holds methods and other statements (see Figure 5.12). If these methods and statements are placed in a Do Together, all of the methods and statements execute simultaneously.

4. The Do Together tiles are located at the bottom of the screen in Figure 5.12. You need to click and drag the tile to the During phase for each event as shown in Figure 5.12.

5. Click on the cow in the object tree. This is so that you can use its methods for the arrow key events that will move the cow object.

6. Drag and drop the cow's walk method to each of the Do Together tiles, as shown in Figure 5.13. This is because whenever the user presses a key you want the cow's legs to move.

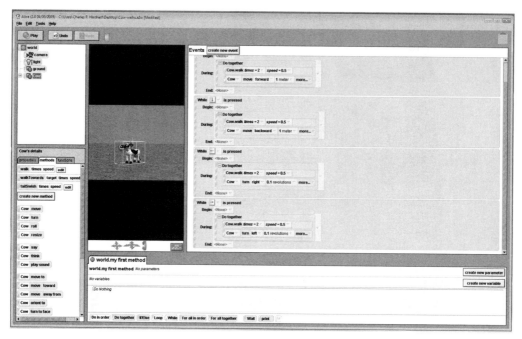

Figure 5.13
All events with the actions for each event dragged to the related event.

7. Drag and drop the cow's move method to the Up and Down arrow key events. The Up arrow key should be Forward and the Down arrow key should be Backward. See Figure 5.13 for where the Up and Down arrow keys have been set. This will allow users to use the Up and Down arrow keys to move the cow forward and backward, respectively.

8. Drag and drop the cow's turn method to the Left and Right arrow key events. The Left key should be Turn Left and the Right arrow key should be Turn Right. Each turn should be set to 0.1 revolutions. See Figure 5.13 for where the Left and Right arrow keys have been set. This will allow the users to turn the cow.

9. Sometimes you need to fine-tune a command/action. To do this, use the More buttons that are provided at the end of each command/action. Typically, you will have the following options to modify:

Duration: The time to execute the command.
Style: The manner in which the action is carried out, such as graceful or abrupt.

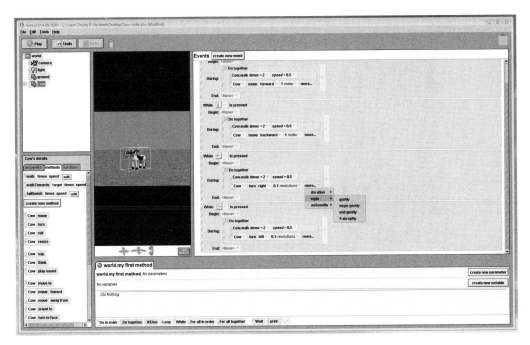

Figure 5.14
This figures depicts the options that are available for most commands under the More option.

As Seen By: This is helpful for turns and rolls so that the turn/roll is done from the perspective of the character instead of the view of the camera.

Figure 5.14 shows how clicking on More reveals a list of options. You need to select Style and then Abruptly.

10. After these steps, the result will look somewhat like the screenshot shown in Figure 5.15. Also, to play with your new navigation controls, you must press the Play button. Have some fun!

Now you have seen several ways to use the keyboard to control the characters of your story. Keep in mind that these are just techniques; you will probably build upon these techniques to provide the unique movement and control that you would like in your virtual world. Next you will take a look at how to move the camera with a main character.

Navigation with the Camera

The camera's viewpoint goes hand in hand with navigation. You might have noticed in the previous examples that, as you moved off the screen, the camera did not follow the character. There are several ways to alleviate this problem.

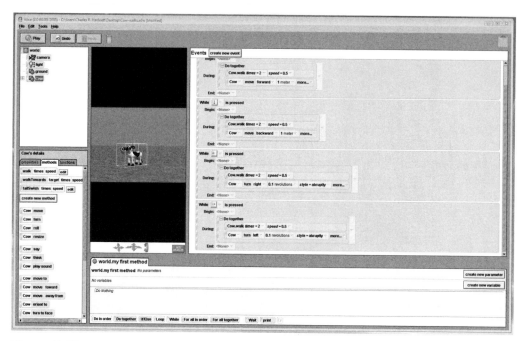

Figure 5.15
This is the final screen for the walking during character navigation.

In this section, I show you two methods that you can use to make the camera follow your main character through your virtual world.

Keeping the Main Character in Frame

The first technique allows you to keep the main character in the center of the camera view. In order to do this in Alice, you have to make the camera move at the same time the main character moves. Because the keyboard controls the main character, the keyboard also controls the camera. The technique used for walking and moving at the same time is the same approach for moving the camera and the character at the same time.

First, you need to create a scene with the Bunny and a few other objects such as trees. An example scene is shown in Figure 5.16 (called out with a 1). The trees in the scene provide perspective when you test how your character turns left and right. The arrow key custom key press events are shown in Figure 5.16 (called out with a 2).

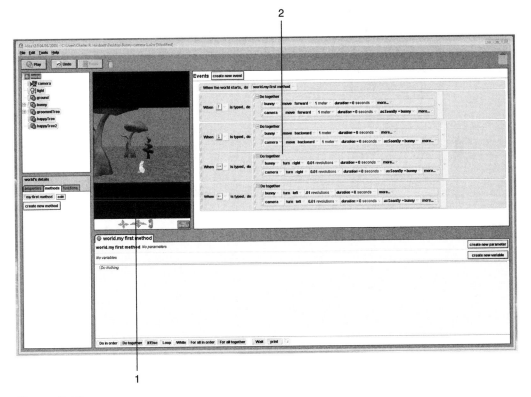

Figure 5.16
The keys must move both the main character and the camera.

Follow these steps to complete this example:

1. Create a new event for the Up arrow key as shown in Figure 5.17. If you do not remember how to do this, see the previous section.

2. Drag Do Together tiles from the bottom of the screen to the During component of each event.

3. Click the bunny in the object tree and drag it into the Do Together tile of the event, as shown in Figure 5.18. The duration must be set to 0 by selecting More for the options. As shown in the figure, select Other.

   Selecting Other will bring up an on-screen number pad, as shown in Figure 5.19. You can then type **0**, and then click Okay. Now this means that this move operation will happen instantaneously.

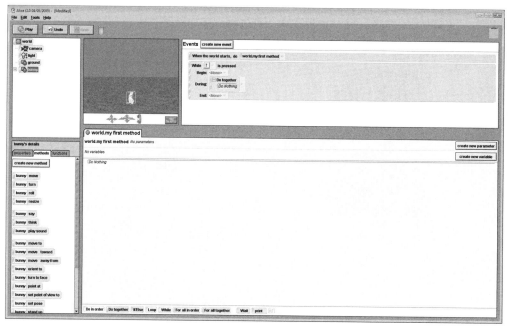

Figure 5.17
The event created for the Up arrow key.

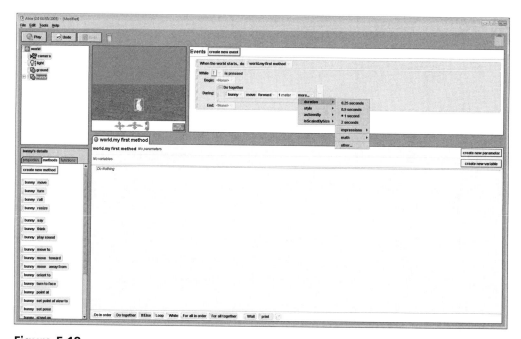

Figure 5.18
This figure shows how the move action for the bunny is added and its duration is changed.

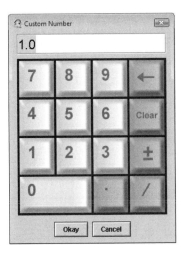

Figure 5.19
The on-screen number pad.

4. Click on the Camera in the object tree, and then drag the move command to the Do Together for the first arrow key event. Select 1 Meter from the pop-up menu. Do not forget the options for duration and asSeenBy. These are key to making the camera move properly. The asSeenBy is set as shown in Figure 5.20. Choose entire bunny from the last menu.

The asSeenBy setting is needed because you want the camera to have the same viewing angle as the bunny. This will make the camera move in the same directions as the bunny. This is not what will put the camera behind the bunny.

5. Now repeat Steps 1–4 for the Down, Right, and Left arrow keys until your results resemble Figure 5.21. The Right and Left arrow keys use a Turn instead of a Move and the number of revolutions of 0.01 is set using Other and the number pad, as was done with Duration in Step 3.

After completing these steps, the camera will follow the bunny. However, the camera will be at its default position, which is at bunny's side. It is usually better to have the camera behind the main character so that the users have a birds-eye view of what is going on in the virtual world.

To do this, you will add instructions to `world.MyFirstMethod`. This is the first method to be launched when the world starts. How do you know this?

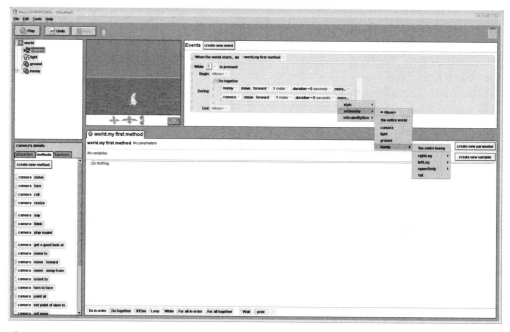

Figure 5.20
The asSeenBy option is used to adjust the orientation of the camera to that of the bunny.

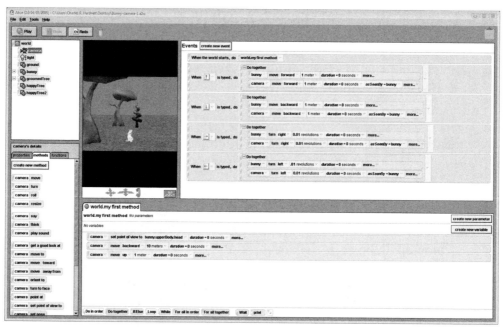

Figure 5.21
All four keyboard events to move the bunny and camera.

If you look at the events in Figure 5.21, notice the first event in the list is called "When the World Starts" and it's connected to the `world.MyFirstMethod` method.

6. To complete this exercise, you will now work on the camera object to set its original camera angle so that it is slightly above the head of the bunny. This will provide a nice view for the users as they move the bunny through the world. Select the Camera object in the object tree. It is currently selected in Figure 5.21. You will now fill in the body of the `world.MyFirstMethod`.

7. Drag and drop the camera's Set Point of View method into the program editing area for the `world.MyFirstMethod`, as shown in the bottom pane of Figure 5.21. The camera should have the point of view of the bunny's head. The Set point of view to command is used to change the initial point of view of the camera to point where the bunny is looking. You can use the entire bunny or just its head.

8. Drag and drop the camera's Move Backward method into the program-editing area for the `world.MyFirstMethod`, as shown in the bottom pane of Figure 5.21. It should be moved backward by 10 meters. This moves the camera so it's behind the bunny.

9. Drag and drop the camera's Move Up method into the program-editing area for the `world.MyFirstMethod`, as shown in the bottom pane of Figure 5.21. It should be moved up by 1 meter.

The final result is shown in Figure 5.22, where you now have a rear view of the bunny and its surroundings.

Keeping the Character in Frame: The Vehicle Method

The previous example showed you how you can use the key pressing events to guide the main character and also the camera. This approach allows you to do various maneuvers and effects with the camera if you desire to do so. There is another way that you can achieve similar results.

The second technique uses the *vehicle property*. This property provides a way of connecting two objects, where one object is the vehicle for the second object. This means that if the first object (the vehicle) moves, the second object would go with it.

Figure 5.23 shows how the vehicle property is used. First, the vehicle in this case is the bunny since the bunny is the character that you can move. To set the

Figure 5.22
The final screen is oriented so it's looking at the back of the bunny and follows the bunny's visual perspective.

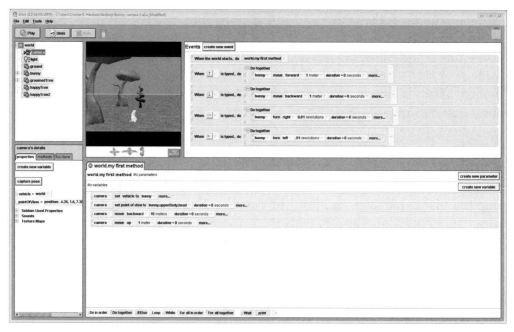

Figure 5.23
The camera follows the bunny using the vehicle property for the camera.

property, you must click on the Camera object, and then from the Details pane, select the Properties tab.

Just drag the vehicle property into the program at the start and place it as shown in Figure 5.23. This is enough. Also note that you can delete the Camera moves and turns from the keyboard events.

This method is easier, but it does not allow you to further manage the camera for special-effect types of movements.

Summary

In this chapter you learned about the various events available to Alice. Some of these events you used extensively in this chapter and others you will use as needed. You also learned how to use the keyboard to navigate your characters around your virtual world. You learned several techniques for achieving this in Alice, which are the foundation for what you need in your virtual world projects. Finally, you learned how to make the camera follow your main character so that your users can see where the character is going and what is in its environment as it moves through the world. Just a reminder that the examples from this chapter are located on the Chapter 5 folder of the accompanying CD.

In the next chapter, you will learn how to program the characters to move around the virtual world. You will learn how to move their arms and legs to make them jump, walk, throw, and more.

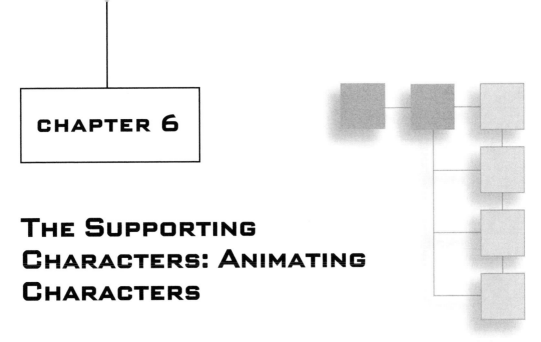

CHAPTER 6

THE SUPPORTING CHARACTERS: ANIMATING CHARACTERS

The previous chapter focused on how to give the user of your world the ability to control the main character with the keyboard. This chapter focuses on showing you how to program characters to move automatically. These characters are typically referred to as *computer-controlled characters* in video games.

The first step to working with computer-controlled characters is to give them simple animation abilities. These abilities give them the appearance of being able to walk, catch, throw, or perform any natural movement.

This chapter focuses on showing you how to make a character make these types of movements, and you will also learn how to make the computer-controlled character follow a pattern to give the appearance of actually doing something in your world. In Chapter 12, you learn how to make these characters follow/chase another character and make them run away from other characters.

Talking Characters

The first animation I show you is very simple, but perhaps one of the most important features for virtual world storytelling and even for games. This feature allows the characters to speak. Now, they won't actually speak (at least not in this chapter), but they will be able to express themselves using text balloons, otherwise known as speech or text bubbles. Text balloons have been around for a very long time, as Figure 6.1 illustrates.

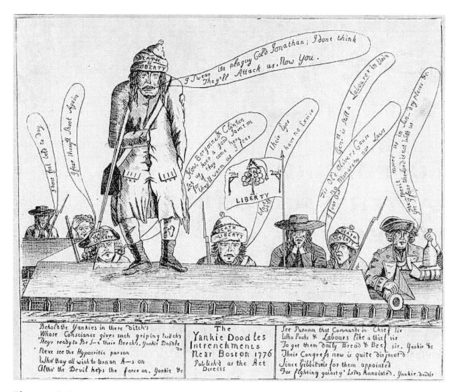

Figure 6.1
An example of text bubbles or speech bubbles. This image is from 1775. Courtesy of Wikipedia (en.wikipedia.org/wiki/Speech_balloon).

You have seen text bubbles on some television shows and commercials. If you read comic strips, you are very familiar with text bubbles. These bubbles have been used for hundreds of years, as shown in Figure 6.1, which shows a cartoon that was drawn in 1775. There is actually a long history related to speech bubbles and their use in cartoons, comic strips, photographs, film, and so on. If you are curious about this history, visit Wikipedia for more information (see http://en.wikipedia.org/wiki/Text_bubble).

Speech Bubbles in Alice

You create speech bubbles in Alice using the Say method, which is available with every Alice object. You can make people and animals talk, or you can make other objects, such as trees, chairs, houses, and so on, talk.

You need to create a new world and add any object from the gallery to your world. After you have done this, your screen will look similar to Figure 6.2.

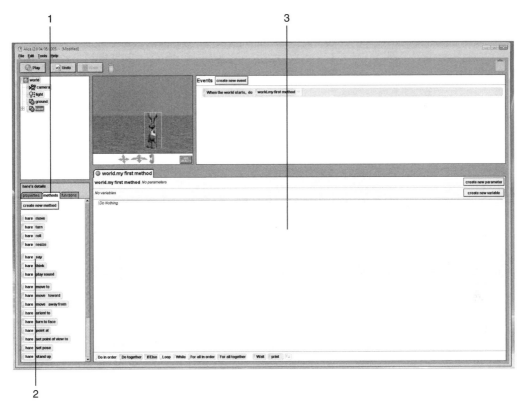

Figure 6.2
An Alice world that shows the methods for the selected object. The Say method is dragged into the program area.

You should focus on the left side, where the list of methods are shown, marked by the callout 1 on Figure 6.2:

1. If your methods are not showing, click on the Methods tab.

2. Scroll down the methods until you see the Say method, as marked by the callout 2 on Figure 6.2.

3. Click and drag the Say method into the program area, as marked by the callout 3 on Figure 6.2.

4. A pop-up menu will appear with some preselected options, such as Hello and Goodbye. You should select Other.

5. Now type the dialogue that you want to show up in the speech bubble.

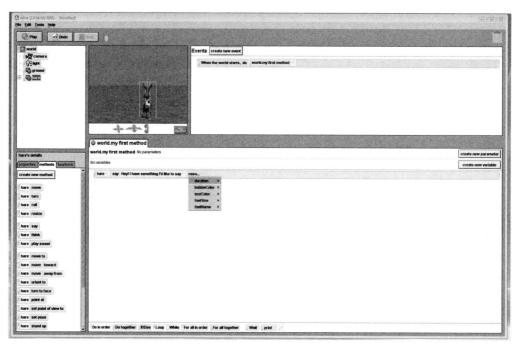

Figure 6.3
This figure shows the pop-up menu for the Say method that allows options to be changed.

If you have done these steps correctly, your world will have a method named Say that contains the words you typed. See Figure 6.3 to compare with what you have done.

By default, the speech bubble will be displayed in a yellow bubble for two seconds. If you want to change the settings, you need to change some options. The following are the options available for the Say method:

- **Duration:** The amount of time to display the bubble.

- **BubbleColor:** The color of the bubble.

- **TextColor:** The color of the text in the bubble.

- **FontSize:** The size of the text in the bubble.

- **FontName:** The font of the text in the bubble.

Let's take some time now and play with some of the options available to alter your bubble:

1. If you have the pop-up menu as shown in Figure 6.3, continue. If not, click the More... area of the Say command. This allows you to get access to the options you just read about.

2. Select a color for the bubble.

3. Select a text color.

4. Click Play to see the results.

5. Change some other options of the Say method and add a few more Say methods to your world.

Speech bubbles are an effective way to provide dialogue in your virtual world, whether it's a game or a short story. I encourage you to use these text bubbles to give depth to your story and to communicate with the users of your game or the viewers of your story. In the next subsection, I show you how you can speak to characters and make them respond.

Communicating with Alice Characters

Now don't get to excited, you will not able to speak to them, but you can use some basic programming concepts to create a conversation between a user and the Alice character in the story. Have you ever heard of a bot? Bots are popular programs found in chat rooms, instant messengers, electronic bulletin boards, and email automated responses. The term bot is short for robot, but in reality, bots are not robots; they are actually software programs. These programs are written in such a way that they can communicate with a human as if they were humans themselves. Consider the following chat room scenario:

You type: "Hello"

Bot responds: "Hello, how are you?"

You type: "I am doing fine; how about yourself?"

Bot responds: "I am doing great; so, what would you like to talk about?"

You type: "Games"

Bot responds: "I love to talk about games."

This type of exchange is very basic and predictable. Therefore, the bot can be programmed to respond to the predictable pattern. In the bot's last response, it even substitutes your word "games" for the activity it loves. However, you can usually deviate from the typical responses and the bot will continue with its typical program. It then becomes obvious that you are not speaking with a human:

You type: "Hello"

Bot responds: "Hello, how are you?"

You type: "I am not feeling well; can you help me?"

Bot responds: "I am doing great; so, what would you like to talk about?"

You type: "I don't really feel like talking too much."

Bot responds: "I love to talk about I don't really feel like talking too much."

In this example, you can see that the responses are not that realistic. The second response from the bot is okay, but not exactly what you would expect since you said you are not feeling well. Then if you look at the third response, it's obvious that the bot is not a person.

In Alice, you can create this type of behavior for your characters. It is good for very simple conversations that have only a few possible answers. In some cases, you can get away with the bot asking questions with only yes/no answers. I will show you two examples of conversational interaction at this time. The first example is very basic like the example of the previous bot, and the second example incorporates a small amount of decision-making.

Basic Conversation

In this example, you will implement the idea shown in the previous subsection where the users and bot have a conversation. To do this, you need to create a new world. Add a person or animal to your world. This character will behave as your bot, so make it a character you don't mind chatting with. The conversation you are going to build is shown in Figure 6.4. I have provided steps here to take you through the process of building this conversation.

Use the following steps to create this basic conversation:

1. Click the Create New Variable button, and name the variable **fromUser**. Select Other and then chose the type to be String. Then click OK. This variable will hold the value of whatever responses the user types.

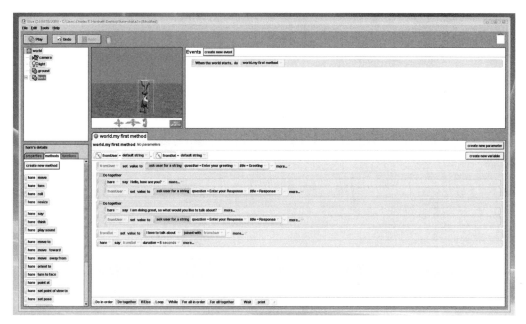

Figure 6.4
This is an example of a bot that can carry out a basic conversation.

2. Drag the fromUser variable to the Do Nothing option, and then select Default Value.

This move creates an assignment to the variable, as seen in Figure 6.5. An *assignment* is how you put values into a variable, and a *variable* is how you can save a value for later use. Whenever you get input from the users, you have to put it in a variable. In this example, you will not use those variables, but in the next example, you will use that input for making decisions.

Now that you have a variable to store the result of asking the users a question, it is time to make your program ask the users to provide a response. There are special functions that belong to the World object to get user input.

3. Select the World from the object tree and then select the Functions tab in the World's Details area. Scroll down until you see the function called Ask User for a String.

4. Drag Ask User for a String to the Default Value of the assignment. A dialog box will appear. Enter the text, **Please enter your greeting**, and then in the next dialog box, type **Hello**.

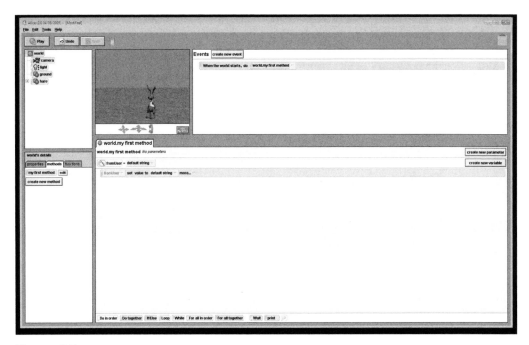

Figure 6.5
This figure shows a newly created variable with a default value.

5. Now select More for this command and select Title and then Other. This title will be the title of the dialog box. Type **Greeting** as the title. See Figure 6.6.

6. Click Play to see how your program is working.

   Now it is time to complete the dialogue. When the character speaks, you want to have the conversation go smoothly and as naturally as possible. You will need to use the Do Together tile so that the users can respond as soon as they finish reading the character's text bubble. Figure 6.7 shows you this part of the conversation within the purple Do Together tile. To create this collection of statements, follow these steps:

7. Click and drag a Do Together tile from the control tiles below to the program area of Alice after the assignment statement.

8. Now select the character in the object tree, and drag a Say method to the Do Together. Select Other from the menu and type **Hello, how are you?**.

9. Drag the fromUser variable to be the next statement in the Do Together. Repeat Steps 3–5 to place the Ask User for a String function, which will ask the users for a response, as shown in Figure 6.7.

Figure 6.6
This figure shows the first part of the dialogue.

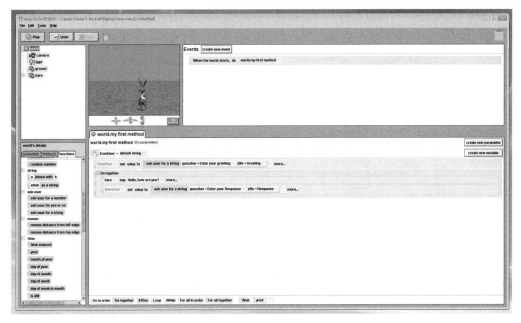

Figure 6.7
The result after adding the second part of the dialogue.

If you have completed all of the steps properly, your program will look like Figure 6.7. You can decide to play it now if you would like to see what it does at this point, or you can proceed to the next phase.

The next phase of this exercise completes the program that allows the Bot character to have a dialogue with the users. Follow these steps to complete the dialogue:

1. If you look back at the dialogue you're creating, you will recall that the bot uses the user's response in the final statement of the dialogue. This is done by appending the user's response string, stored in the fromUser variable, to the beginning part of the bot's final statement. This is what you will learn to do now.

2. Click on the Create New Variable button. Select a String type and name the variable **fromBot**.

3. Drag fromBot down below the Do Together, as shown in Figure 6.8.

4. Click on the World object in the object tree and then click on the Functions tab in Details. Scroll down until you find the a Joined with b function. This function appends string b onto the end of string a.

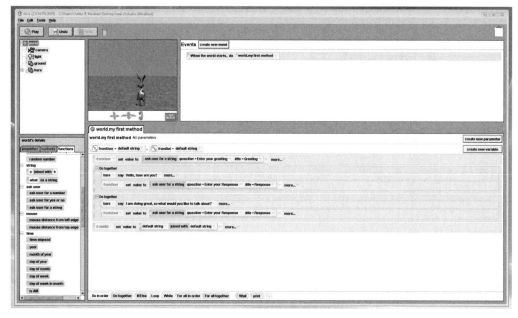

Figure 6.8
Shows the third part of the dialogue and the use of "a Joined with b".

The a Joined with b function allows you to take the input from the user and allow the Bot character to use those same words. This will be done by having the "a" be the words for the bot and "b" will be the users' responses about what they like to talk about.

5. Drag the a Joined with b function to the Default String and fill in the first part of the "join with" with the phrase "I love to talk about" and the second part will use the fromUser variable.

   Now you have stored the bot's response into a variable called fromBot. You can use this to finish this program, as shown in Figure 6.9.

6. Select your character in the object tree, and then find the Say method. Drag the Say method into position, and then select the Expressions and select fromBot from the drop-down list.

7. Notice in Figure 6.9 that the last statement is set to execute with a duration of 20 seconds. This was done because it's the last statement and if it goes by too fast you will not get to see the result of your handy work.

The program you just created shows an example of how you can program a character to have a very simple conversation with the users. Since the users can

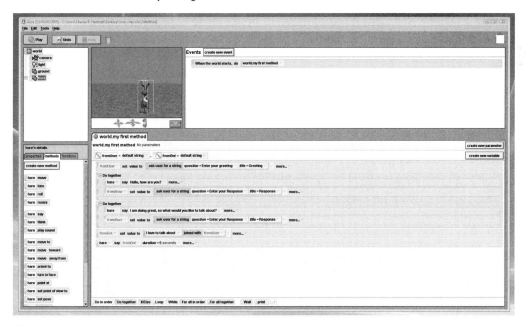

Figure 6.9
This figure shows the finished program that shows how to perform the dialogue presented earlier in the chapter.

enter anything that means the conversation can be different each time. Now, of course the character does not understand the conversation. However, it is possible to make your character make decisions based on what the user types. Doing this will increase the level of interactivity in your projects.

Advanced Conversation: Making Decisions

The conversation you implemented in the previous section was basic and does not allow your bot to make decisions abut how to react based on responses. This requires that you add some logic to the bot for making decisions. In Alice, you have one basic option that allows you to make decisions and it's called the *IfElse*. The IfElse works like the following:

If *it's raining*

   Take your umbrella

Else

   Leave your umbrella

The IfElse allows you to examine a True/False condition and then make a decision about which action to perform. In a conversation the True/False condition is based on the response from the users. For example, consider the following conversation:

Bot: "What's up?"

User: "Not much"

Bot's logic:

   If User does not say "busy"

     Say "That's great, let's play a game!"

   Else

     Say "Oh, you're busy, maybe later"

Bot: "That's great, let's play a game!"

To create this example, you need to create a new world with one character placed in it from the gallery. To create this new dialogue, follow these steps:

1. Create a new variable called **fromUser**.

Figure 6.10
This shows the first part of the dialogue that is similar to the basic dialogue examples.

2. Add a Do Together tile similar to the one in the previous section where the bot speaks and waits for the users to respond. If you do not remember how to do this, you should the review the steps in the previous section. Your program should look like the one shown in Figure 6.10.

   To complete the dialogue, you have to add the IfElse to provide the logic for the bot to make a decision about how to respond to the user. These next steps will finish the program, as shown in Figure 6.11.

3. Click and drag the IfElse tile to be positioned after the Do Together. Choose True from the pop-up menu.

4. Drag the fromUser variable to True. You will be shown fromUser == and fromUser !=. Use the fromUser != option and then select Other and type **Busy**.

   The comparison symbols are == (equal to) and != (not equal to).
   The logic in this example determines whether the user responds with "Busy".

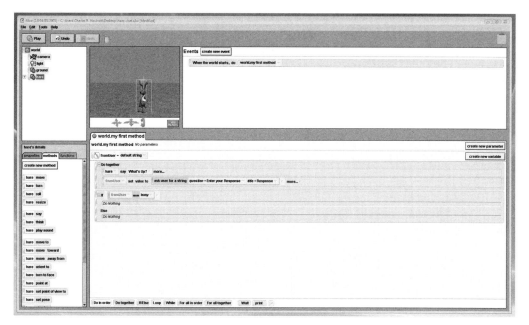

Figure 6.11
This shows the completed dialogue with the decision-making statements set up for the bot.

5. Click on your Alice character in the object tree (I chose the hare again). Drag the Say method to both parts of the IfElse, as shown in Figure 6.11.

6. Click on the Play button to see what happens!

In this section, you explored various ways to give users the illusion that they are communicating with the Alice character. You also were introduced to the IfElse statement, which allows you to incorporate decision-making abilities within your programs. You will be shown other uses of the IfElse statement in other chapters. In the next section, you learn how to move body parts of a character to simulate actions, such as walking!

Animating Characters: Learning to Walk

Animating the characters in Alice is what gives more realism to the virtual worlds you create. If your characters were moving around, but not actually moving the legs and arms as if they were walking, it would appear that everyone has their own private hovercraft or something. Walking can be a complex task to achieve in Alice, and so you will learn walking at the end this section. However, you will explore various movements that lead nicely into walking. You will start off by learning some basic movements for arms and legs. You will learn how to make characters do something like give a high-five or shake hands. You will learn how to make a character jump. Finally, you'll put all of this together to give the character the ability to walk.

Learning to Move Arms

The first concept to understand about animating characters in Alice is the fact that the characters are a composition of objects. This is shown in the object tree of Figure 6.12. You can see in the figure how the girl is broken down into three major parts: body, leftLeg, and rightLeg. These parts are further broken down where you can see that legs are made up of lowerLegs and a foot, whereas the body has the arms and neck attached. The arms have forearms and hands, whereas the neck has the head.

As the programmer in Alice, you have control over each one of these sub-objects that make up the girl object in this case. If you click on any of these sub-objects you will see that it has a list of methods, properties, and functions in the details section, just like the girl object. This is the power that you will exploit in order to

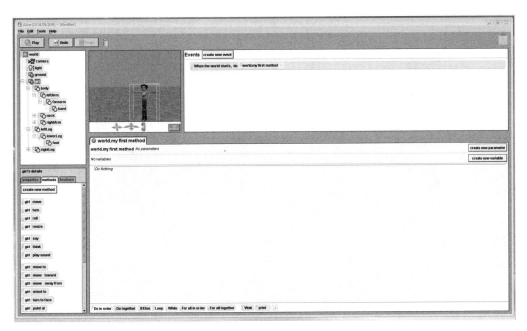

Figure 6.12
The girl character added to the scene and the object tree for the girl.

animate the various parts of the characters in Alice. It should be noted that not all people characters have the exact same breakdown and that animals and other creatures will have similar, but not the same, breakdowns. Therefore, you should get to know the characters you are working with and assess how much control you have over parts of their bodies before you commit to using them in your virtual world.

Moving Arms Down

Moving arms is a good place to start because many of the human characters you add to Alice will be added with their arms up like the girl in Figure 6.12. Moving arms up and down requires the Roll method for the arms. There are two ways that this can be accomplished. You can do this in the design mode or in the programming mode. In both modes, you will use the Roll method. The Roll method is used because it is used to turn an object left and right on center point. In the case of an arm, the center point is the shoulder. This means that when you roll the arm left or right, it will swivel into the body or away from the body.

The design mode is where you have to use the arm object to access the roll method. Figure 6.13 shows how to move the person's arms down to the side

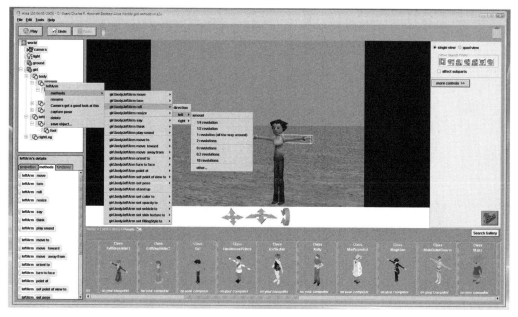

Figure 6.13
This shows how to move a person's arms down to the side.

using the arm object submenus. Remember that all objects in Alice have these same submenus. To do this, try the following:

1. Select the + symbol next to the girl object in the object tree. This will expand the girl object and reveal its sub-objects.

2. Select the + symbol next to the Body object. Now you will see the leftArm objects.

3. Right-click on the leftArm object to reveal the submenu for the leftArm object. Follow the submenu selections, as shown in Figure 6.13, to get to the Roll method.

4. Choose left and 1/4 revolution.

5. Repeat Steps 3 and 4 for the rightArm object and roll right.

6. Choose the Properties tab under the object tree. Select the girl in the object tree.

7. Click the Capture Pose button and name the pose ArmsAtSide. You can then use this positioning later when you build the walk for the girl.

As a reminder, the 1/4 (quarter) revolution is like moving 1/4 of the way around a circle. In this case, the arm will move left (clockwise) a quarter of a circle. This causes the arm to move downward. Here are details for how rolls work:

- **Roll Left:** Clockwise roll around the axis indicating the direction the character is facing.

- **Roll Right:** Counter-clockwise roll around the axis indicating the direction the character is facing.

Therefore, if the character is facing you, its arms will spin around the z-axis. If the character is facing the left or right, the arms will rotate around the x-axis. There is another way that you could do this same thing with characters initially. When you add a character to the world you can fix the arms to make them go down to the side.

Every object and sub-object can be controlled by methods in the design mode as shown in Figure 6.13. The advantage of using the design mode is that the character is preset this way and you don't have to program them to have their arms down.

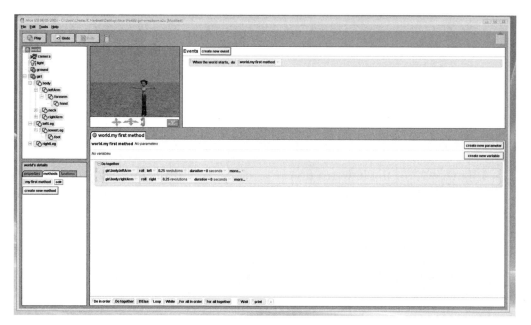

Figure 6.14
This shows how you can move the arms down during the scene setup phase.

If you want to, you can use the programming mode instead. A program that moves the arms down for the girl object is shown in Figure 6.14. Usually, you will do this type of programming at the start of your world so that all of the characters' arms are moved down at the same time and you don't have to do all the clicking that you have to do in design mode if you have a large number of characters. The following steps will lead you through developing this program that is shown in Figure 6.14:

1. Drag and drop the Do Together tile from the bottom of the Editing pane to inside the Editing pane.

2. Select the + symbol next to the girl object in the object tree. This will expand the girl object and reveal its sub-objects.

3. Select the + symbol next to the Body object. Now you will see the leftArm objects.

4. Select the leftArm object and then select the Methods tab.

5. Scroll down to find the Roll method and drag it into the Do Together structure you just placed in the program.

6. Set the Roll method to a quarter revolution of the left arm.

7. Follow Steps 4-6 to roll the right arm.

Moving the arms down is a prerequisite for being able to make a character walk. The first method allows you to save a pose of the character that is useful for walking. The second method is easier to duplicate in your program to set several characters and you can use the method for moving the arms in other ways just by changing the number of revolutions. If you do not intend on adding a walking feature to all of your characters, the second method is the best way to go.

Moving the Upper Body

One of the goals of this chapter is to program a character to walk. When the character walks, it's important that the arms move back and forth like a pendulum. In addition, you have to move the torso and head. In general, your torso and head rotate towards the arm coming forward. So the plan will be to do the following steps at the same time.

Do together:

- Turn torso to the left

- Turn head to the left

- Move left arm forward and right arm backward

Do together:

- Turn torso to the right

- Turn head to the right

- Move left arm backward and right arm forward

If you put these steps in a loop, you will have the basis for creating the upper body's "walking" movements. In Alice, you have to change the options for duration and style. These changes are to shorten the duration of the movements and to create a more natural movement.

Before you can create the program that will do the steps discussed here, you need to create a Pose in Alice for the positions of your character's arms. A pose in Alice is similar to a person "striking a pose" for the camera. To create a pose, you should be in design mode:

1. In design mode, you can use the object tree to select the UpperLeftArm of the girl, or of your character. Select the effected subparts from the toolbox.

Tip

Zooming in design mode can be very useful for activities like this. This will allow you to see what you are doing more easily. First you need to enter the Quad-View. Then there will be a magnifying glass icon added to the toolbox. Second, select the magnifying glass icon from the toolbox. Now your mouse can allow you to zoom in and out. Finally, click and drag the mouse on the Front-View pane. Moving the mouse up and down zooms in and out respectively.

2. Then use the toolbox tool, called Turnable Objects, to move the arm so that it is moving in front of the character, as shown in Figure 6.15. (Note that I also had to move the lower part of the arm to get a good form.)

3. Then select the rightArm of the character and move it back; this is also shown in Figure 6.15. I also had to move the lower part of the arm as well to get a good form so that it appears that her arm is slightly bent.

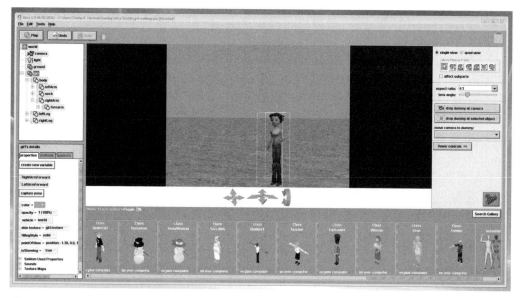

Figure 6.15
This shows how you set and capture a pose in the design mode.

4. Now click the Capture Pose button (if you don't see it, choose the Properties tab first). This will save the positioning. Give the pose a name that you can remember. I used **LeftArmForward**.

5. Repeat Steps 1–4 to place the right arm forward. Call the pose **RightArmForward**.

Now you will use these poses to help create the bolded parts of the algorithm that was presented earlier in the section.

Do together:

- Turn torso to the left

- Turn head to the left

- Move left arm forward and right arm backward

Do together:

- Turn torso to the right

- Turn head to the right

- Move left arm backward and right arm forward

The following steps will explain how to create the program you see in Figure 6.16:

1. Drag and drop the Loop tile from the collection of control structures to the programming area. Set the loop to 2 Times. The loop tile is what will make the arms swing continuously forward and backward.

2. Drag and drop two Do Together tiles in the loop. The Do Together tiles are used to control the movement where the left arm is moved forward and the right arm backward, and vice-versa. There is one Do Together for each combination.

3. Select the girl object from the object tree and drag and drop Set Pose method to the first Do Together and set it to LeftArmForward pose.

4. Change the options of the Set Pose by selecting the More... part of the method; change the style to Abruptly and the duration to 0.5 seconds. This will make the movement of the arms very smooth. You will use these settings for all of the movements.

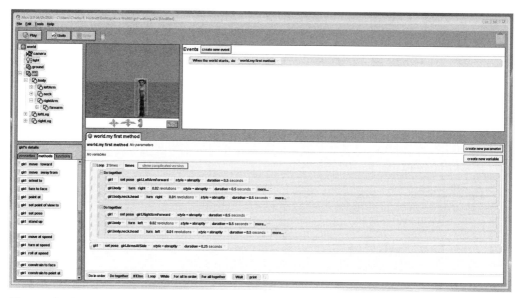

Figure 6.16
This shows the program that will make your character swing its arms in a walking motion.

5. Expand the girl object in the object tree like it is shown in Figure 6.16. Then select the body object of the girl object.

6. Drag the turn method for the body object into the first Do Together. Set it to turn right for 0.2 revolutions. Also, set its style and duration using the More... part of the method.

7. Select the head object of the girl object, and drag the turn method into the first Do Together. Set it to turn right for 0.1 revolutions. Then, set its style and duration using the More... part of the method.

Your program should have the Loop structure and the first completed Do Together, as shown in Figure 6.16. To finish the program, you need to do the following:

1. Repeat the previous Steps 3–7, but this time, use the RightArmForward pose and you move the Body and Head objects to the left. This will complete the second Do Together.

2. Select the girl object and drag the Set Pose method after the Loop structure. Set the pose for ArmsAtSide. This will just end the arm swinging with her arms comfortably at her side.

You have finished the program for moving the upper body for walking. To recap, the style is chosen to be Abruptly because it makes the movements more natural looking. The other style settings make the movement appear to be in slow motion. The durations and revolutions are created by trial-and-error. They are a good start, but you may find that you need to adjust these values if you want a different effect or if you are using a different character. The poses are created to simplify the building of the upper-body movements. You could have steps to move the arms instead of setting poses, but it's more complicated. In the next section, you will work on the lower body.

Moving the Lower Body

Now that you have the upper body working, you can focus on learning to move the lower body. You'll move the lower body in a similar fashion as you did the upper body. Just like with the upper body, you will have two options for working with the lower body. However, this section will only explore the option of setting poses in the design mode. Then you will use these poses to perform the walking motion in the program. The steps for moving the lower body are the following:

Do together:

- Right leg halfway forward and left leg halfway back

- Character moves some small amount forward

Do together:

- Right leg full extension and left leg back fully

- Character moves some small amount forward

Do together:

- Left leg halfway forward and right leg halfway back

- Character moves some small amount forward

Do together:

- Left leg full extension and right leg back fully

- Character moves some small amount forward

To implement this in Alice, you need to build the poses. There are four poses required that correspond with the previous algorithm.

Creating a pose with the lower body involves using the same method you used for moving arms (the Turn method is built into all Alice objects). You will need to do this in the design mode, with the Affect Subparts option checked in the toolbox, and you may need Quad-View in some occasions. Here is an example that creates the pose for right leg halfway forward and left leg halfway back:

1. Click the + signs next to the girl object and her sub-objects until you reach the rightLowerLeg and leftLowerLeg.

2. Select the rightUpperLeg in the object tree.

3. Right-click on the rightUpperLeg to reveal the menu, and follow the Methods menu to the Turn method. Choose forward and 0.1 revolution. This will give the upper-right leg a slight bend forward. See Figure 6.17 for an example of how this will look when all of the menus are expanded.

4. Right-click on the rightLowerLeg to reveal the menu, and follow the Methods menu to the Turn method. Choose backward about 0.05

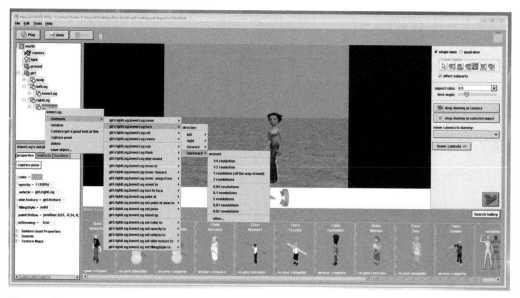

Figure 6.17
The object tree object pop-up menu for the leg of the character.

revolutions. This will complete the right leg and it will appear she is just starting to lift her right leg to step forward.

5. Right-click on the leftLowerLeg to reveal the same menu, and follow the Methods to the turn method. Choose to turn backward about 0.05 revolutions. This will make it appear that she is starting to push off of her left leg.

6. Select the girl in the object tree, and then the Properties tab in the details pane. Click the Capture pose button and name the pose RightHalfForward. The first pose is complete.

7. Now use these steps to complete pose for RightFullForward by turning the lower-right leg further out so that the leg is almost straight. You will do this by using turn forward on the lower-right leg about another 0.05 revolutions.

8. Then turn the upper-left leg backward about 0.05 revolutions.

9. Create the pose for RightFullFoward.

10. Use these steps to create the poses for LeftHalfForward and LeftFullForward. You can adjust the turns slightly one way or the other to make the walk you would like to have. You can also use Figure 6.18 as a guide to see how each pose should look.

After you have saved your poses, you can complete the more difficult part of walking. Now I want to discuss the ambiguous statements that state small

Figure 6.18
Shows the four poses for the girl's legs: RightHalfForward, RightFullForward, LeftHalfForward, LeftFullForward.

amount forward. The small amount forward is not quite enough information to make a program; you need a distance that is more precise. To figure this out, you need to start by determining how far you want the character to move in one step. This is like determining the character's stride. For example, assume that you want the character to move 0.5 meters in one step (roughly 20 inches). You will need to solve for the small amount to move forward on each of the four moves (0.5/4 = 0.125 meters). This means that you will move 0.125m each time the leg moves.

Now that you should understand that part of the algorithm, you can write the program that moves the lower body. The program is shown in Figure 6.19. The program is fairly easy to write and follows the pseudocode exactly. The only exceptions were the exact timing duration and the distance moved by the character during one step, which you just read about. Build the program according to the figure (refer back to the section "Moving the Upper Body" to recall how to put the Do Together blocks into the program with the Loop block). Now play the character and watch her walk.

Now you have completed the lower body of the walk. With the upper body of the walk complete and the lower body complete, you are ready to put them together to have a fully walking person. This is the topic of the next section.

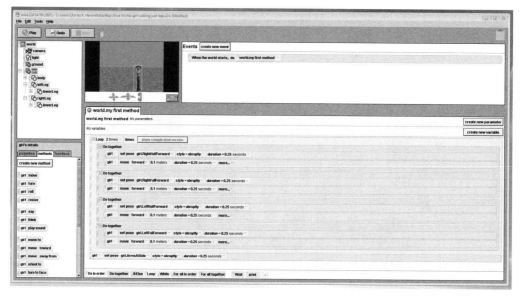

Figure 6.19
This figure shows the program for moving the girl's legs.

Putting the Lower Body and Upper Body Code Together

Now you are ready to make the character walk. The coordinated movement of the arms and legs produces a smooth walking motion. In this section, you will create a new method for your characters that enables you to have them walk at anytime. The new method can be used in your virtual world just like any of the other methods Alice already provides. After you have completed this new method you will be able to simply tell the girl to walk, and she will start walking.

The method that you are going to create is shown in Figure 6.20. In this figure, you will see parts that resemble the programs you wrote to move the arms and legs in the two previous sections named "Moving the Upper Body" and "Moving the Lower Body". Notice how the Do Together for moving the left arm is coupled with moving the right leg. If you think about how you walk, you will see that this is exactly how you keep your balance. When you move your left leg forward, you move your right arm forward; and when you move your right leg forward, you move your left arm forward.

This idea is reflected in the Walk method shown in Figure 6.20. To create the new Walk method, you can follow these steps:

1. Select your character from the object tree and select the Methods tab from the details. Finally, click the Create New Method button. Name the

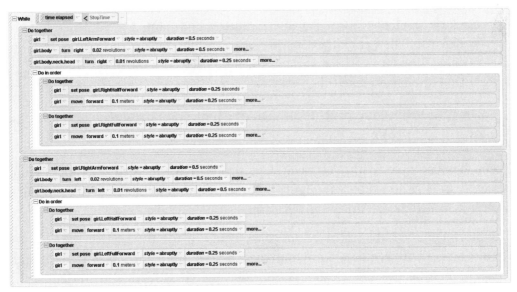

Figure 6.20
This figure shows a new method called Walk that was created for the girl object.

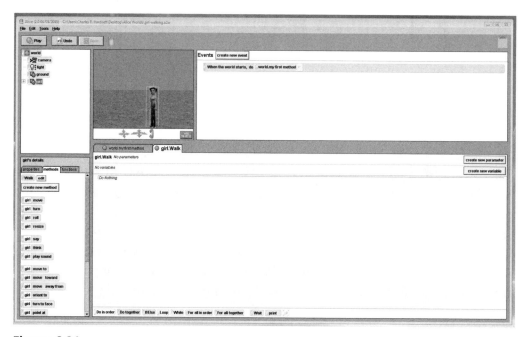

Figure 6.21
This figure shows a new method called Walk that was created for the girl object.

method **Walk**. This will open a new tab in the program pane, as shown in Figure 6.21.

2. Click on the Create New Parameter button and name the parameter WalkTime. Then click the Create New Variable button and name the variable StopTime. These variables will be used to control the duration of time the character walks.

3. Drag the While loop control tile from the bottom of the screen into position over the Do Nothing body.

If you have completed the last two steps properly, your Walk method should resemble the method shown in Figure 6.22. So you should have a While loop tile, a variable called Stop Time, and a parameter called Walk Time.

The Stop Time variable must be set to be equal to the time when the walking should stop. This requires knowing the current time for the virtual world. Imagine that there is a clock that starts when the virtual world is started. If the virtual world has been running for 30 seconds, the clock's current time is 30 seconds. If the world has been running for two minutes, current time is

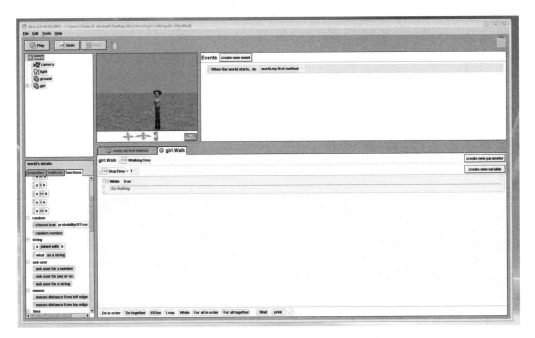

Figure 6.22
The status of the program after adding the parameter, variable, and main loop.

2 minutes. The Stop Time is then the current time plus the amount of walking time. So if the character started walking at current time equal to 30 seconds and it should walk for 15 seconds, and then it should stop at 30 seconds + 15 seconds, which equals 45 seconds. The next few steps will show you how to perform this operation.

1. Drag the variable StopTime to the area above the While loop. This will bring up a pop-up menu; select Set Value from the menu, and then select Expressions, and then Stop Time. This will look strange because you are setting the variable to itself.

2. Drag the parameter Walking Time to the second Stop Time from the previous step. Now you have a command that sets Stop Time to the value of Walking Time. There is still work to be done to get this expression where the elapsed time is added to the walking time.

3. Use the menu shown in Figure 6.23 as a guide for this step. Click on the Walking Time variable to see the pop-up menu. Choose the Math option, which allows you to build expressions with basic math operators for addition, subtraction, multiplication, and division. Select the Addition option

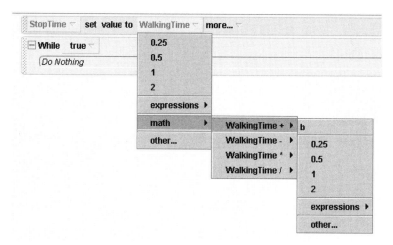

Figure 6.23
The menus that create the addition expression.

and then the value of 1 or any value. The value is a placeholder, and in the next step you will replace it with elapsed time.

4. Now your command has Walking Time + 1 in it. The 1 is a placeholder for the current time; in Alice the current time is found by using the function *time elapsed*. This function gives the time from the start of the Alice program to the current point in time.

5. Select the world object from the object tree, and then select the Functions tab. Scroll down to find the Time Elapsed function.

6. Drag the Time Elapsed function to replace that value you added to WalkTime. In my case, I am replacing the 1. Your method should resemble Figure 6.24.

7. Use the Walk method shown in Figure 6.25 to include the movement of the arms and the standing pose of the character. Note that this code is the same as you created in the "Moving the Upper Body" section of this chapter.

8. Update the Walk method by adding the instructions for moving the legs, as shown in Figure 6.26. This is the same code that was used in the moving lower body section. As a reminder, this is done by first putting in the Do In Order tiles in each of the Do Togethers first. This is so the legs will move at the same time as the arms. After that you can put the two Do Togethers for the right leg on the top and for the left leg on the bottom.

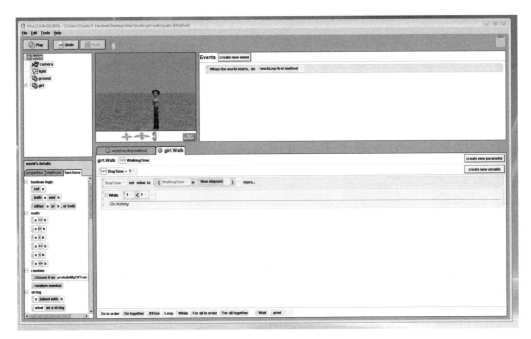

Figure 6.24
The Stop Time is properly set before the While loop.

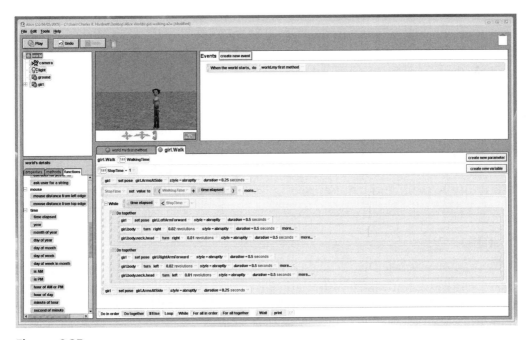

Figure 6.25
This figure shows the body of the loop in the Walk method after the arms movement has been added.

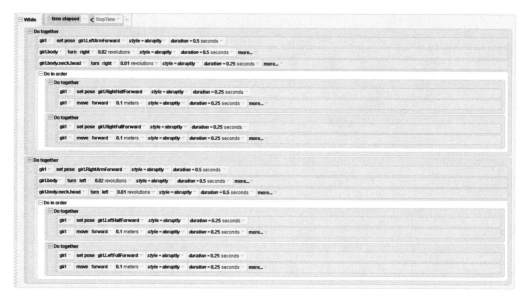

Figure 6.26
This figure shows the body of the loop that should be in your Walk method when it is complete.

Note: Be sure the left arm is moving with the right leg and the right arm is moving with the left leg or else your character will appear off-balance.

Learning to walk is something that you and I learned as toddlers, and our parents had to help us. In similar fashion, you have to teach your characters to walk as well. This seems like a long exercise, but if you go back through these instructions each time you need to teach a character to walk, you will get the hang of it. In addition, you can use the function in conjunction with the keyboard controls used in Chapter 5 to make your main character walk. In fact, remember in Chapter 5, you chose the cow object from the gallery because it had the ability to walk already. Now with your new method, this character has the ability to walk and can be used in the same way! That is really cool!

Summary

This chapter was filled with new concepts. The goal was to learn how to make characters move body parts automatically to play supporting roles in your virtual world. You started by making the characters speak and have a real conversation with the users. The chapter then explored how to move parts of the character's upper body and lower body. You then took the ideas for upper body and lower body and put them together to create a walking method. You can use the techniques in this chapter to create movements such as handshakes, throwing motions, jumping motions, or even running! You should spend some time developing some of the poses for these motions and put them together to create custom functions. Okay, take a deep breath, have some fun with these techniques, and then go on to Chapter 7!

As with other chapters, the CD contains examples taken from this chapter that you can use to help you better understand these concepts and to provide examples to play with to learn more.

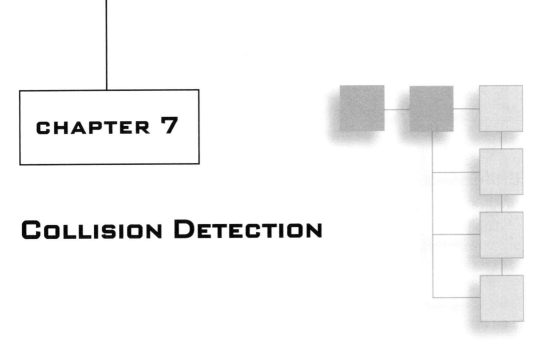

CHAPTER 7

COLLISION DETECTION

Collision detection is very important to any virtual world programmer. *Collision detection* is where a program determines whether two or more objects have intersected with each other. Collision detection is used in virtual worlds to determine whether a character is walking into a particular area of the world or picking up an object. In games, collision detection is used to determine whether a player has achieved a goal in the game. For example, successfully shooting an enemy, or successfully collecting an object in the game that gives the player special powers or points. There are many examples where objects in virtual worlds come in contact with one another, and therefore cause a collision.

Collision detection is a popular topic in gaming communities, and there are several methods that are used for collision detection in games. Some of these methods include the *bounding box* and *bounding sphere* methods. These methods use an imaginary box or sphere that encloses each object in the world. The goal for collision detection is to determine whether the imaginary shape of one object intersects with the imaginary shape of another object. There are other more sophisticated techniques available and others being developed all of the time.

Alice provides methods that can be used for collision detection that are built into every Alice object. In this chapter, you learn to use these methods to determine how close or how far away objects are from each other. These methods are available to you to use in many different ways. This chapter gives you an introduction to these methods and covers some common ways in which they have been used for solving collision-detection problems. In addition, the latter part of the chapter provides some direction in developing other custom collision-detection methods.

Understanding Basic Collision Detection

In Alice, the methods provided for collision detection are considered *proximity* functions. These functions work best with smaller objects rather than larger objects. This is because these proximity functions measure the distance between the two objects by using the distance between the center points. Another factor that affects the effectiveness of the proximity functions is the shape of the objects. If the objects are uniform in shape—such as circles, spheres, cubes, or squares—the proximity functions work very well. However, if they have a more oblong shape like an oval or a rectangle, the proximity functions are far less effective.

Figure 7.1(a) shows three small circles that could represent three marbles or balls in Alice. The center points for these two objects are very close to the surface of the objects and they are roughly the same size. Regardless of where the objects intersect, the distance between the center points will be less than some value. These situations are very good for the proximity functions in Alice. However, in Figure 7.1(b) there is an undesirable situation where the intersection at one part of the rectangle is a much shorter distance to the center object as opposed to another part of the rectangle. The short and long arrows in the figure show this.

The problem here is that if you choose to use the shorter distance, *length = x*, as your measure for determining a collision, the collision shown by the distance

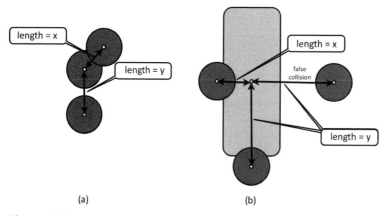

(a)   (b)

Figure 7.1
Examples of different size objects colliding.

length = *y* will not be detected. On the other hand, if you choose the longer distance, *length* = *y*, as the threshold for the collision detection, both collisions involving *length* = *x* and *length* = *y* will be detected. Unfortunately, false detections will be found as well because the shape does not have a uniform distance from its center point; and therefore, the distance, *length* = *y*, will be met even when the circle object is not touching the rectangle object when approaching it on the long side of the rectangle. Now, you are ready to explore some examples.

Ball Bouncing on the Head

This example is where you will see how to detect collisions between small objects and people and animals. Typically, the people and animals in Alice are composed of several smaller objects such as the head and hands. Therefore, based on the previous explanation, it is in your best interest to consider detecting collisions between some small object such as a ball and a part of the person or animal; in this case, it's the head of the person.

Figure 7.2 shows the design of the world you need to create for this example. You can use any of the worlds with a ground such as the grass world used here. Then

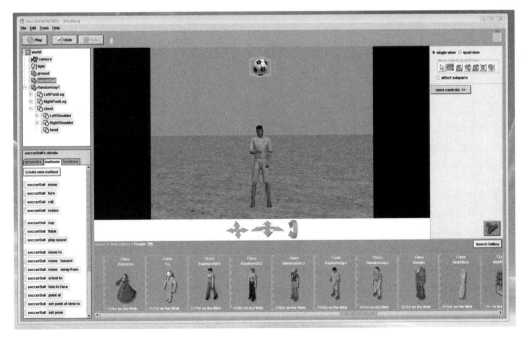

Figure 7.2
The design mode for this world includes the RandomGuy object and the soccerBall object.

you need to add the RandomGuy and soccerBall objects to the world in the arrangement, as shown in the figure.

Click on the Add objects button and then use the Gallery to find the RandomGuy in the people collection and the soccer ball in the Sports collection. Add each object to the world and position them as shown in Figure 7.2. Once you have completed the setup, follow these steps to create your first virtual world program with collision detection:

1. Select the While tile from the bottom of the screen and drag it into the program area over the Do Nothing. Choose the True condition, as this will be replaced in the next step. The True condition is the Boolean expression's default and determines if the While loop should keep looping. A Boolean expression is an expression that compares values such as "1 < 10". If "1" is less than 10, the expression is True; otherwise it's False. A While loop will stop when the expression is false. Therefore, using True there means the loop will never stop.

2. Select the soccerBall object in the object tree, and then select the Functions tab in the Details view.

3. Select the Is At Least function and drag it over the True in the While loop. You can then select the object and distance. The object should be the RandomGuy object's head and the distance should be 0.5 meters. You can check what you have against Figure 7.3, which shows the function in place where it can stop the loop.

   This is the collision detection needed for this exercise. The loop will stop when the ball is close enough to the head to be considered a collision. The next steps are needed to move the ball and make it appear to bounce off the guy's head.

4. Figure 7.4 shows how to move the ball down on the screen within the loop at a 0.1 fraction of a meter. First, you have to drag and drop the Loop tile into the program area, and then drag your While loop into that Loop tile. Change the loop times from infinity to 10 times.

5. Select soccerBall from the object tree, and then select the Methods tab of the Details pane. Scroll down to the Move method. Drag and drop the Move method, as you see in Figure 7.4, into the body of the loop. This move will be set to move down 0.1 meters.

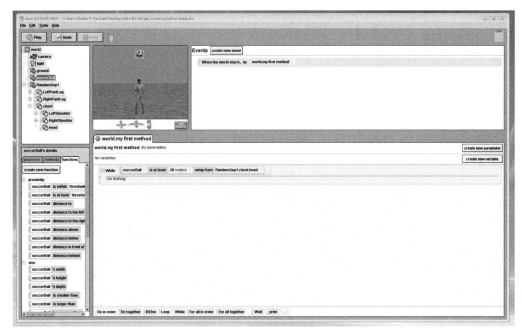

Figure 7.3
The While loop with the threshold condition.

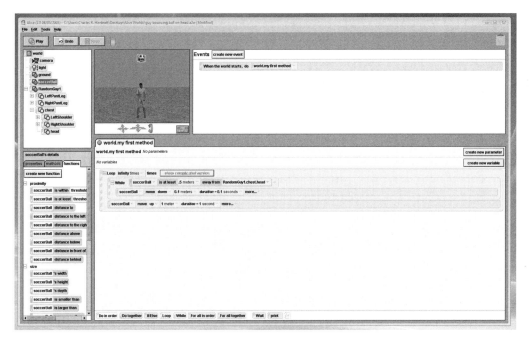

Figure 7.4
This figure shows how to fill in the loop to move the ball.

The While loop says "While the ball has not reached the guy's head, move down 0.1 meters at a time".

To make the ball bounce, it has to move back to the original position. The problem now is with moving back up. The easy solution is to realize that if the loop executes 10 times and each time the ball moves down 0.1 meters, the ball would have traveled 1 meter.

6. Drag and drop a Move method after the While loop, as shown in Figure 7.4. This will move the ball back up to its original position, 1 meter above the guy's head.

7. Click Play to see the result.

   Notice that the ball does repel when it gets to the guy's head and it appears to be bouncing on his head. This program works only if we know the ball is only going to be 1 meter above his head. However, suppose you want a program where you can change the starting position of the ball and the program will still work without any other modifications? You will need variables that can hold the positions of the ball: the ball's starting position and ending position. With these two values, you can determine how far the ball fell by subtracting the ending position from the starting position. This will be distance to move the ball back up to give the appearance of bouncing. Remember the key here is that the new program is generic for any starting position, whereas the previous program only works for when the ball starts 1 meter above the guy's head. Let's see how this is done.

8. Click the Create New Variable button and a dialog box will appear like the one shown in Figure 7.5. In the dialog box, name the variable **Start Position**. Its type should be Other: Position. This type is used to store the (X, Y, Z) coordinates that indicate an object's position. This variable will save the starting position of the ball.

9. Create another variable and call it **End Position**. It should have the same characteristics as Start Position. This variable will record the ending position of the ball after it comes into contact with the guy's head.

10. Select the soccerBall object from the object tree and select Functions in the Details view. Drag the Start Position variable into the program before the Loop tile. Select the default vector to save to the position.

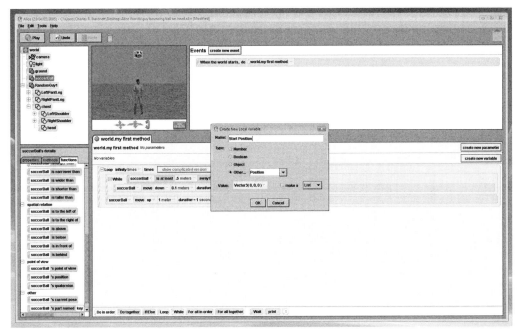

Figure 7.5
Adding a variable that saves a position.

This is done so that you can have a place to save the start position of the ball before you start to move the ball in the loop. It must be done before entering the loop because the loop is going to change the ball's position.

11. Scroll to find the soccerBall's Position in its list of functions and place it over the default vector. Your program should now look like Figure 7.6. Do the same for the End Position variable after the While loop has completed.

   The ball will stop only when it comes in contact with the guy's head. Therefore, it is time for the ball to repel upward and the While loop will end. At this point in time, the ball has reached its ending position.

12. Change the distance for the Move Up by dragging and dropping the End Position variable over the 1 Meter distance. You can select any of the End Position values from the pop-up menu.

   Remember building an addition expression in Chapter 6? You did that to determine when the character should stop walking. In this case, you will build a subtraction expression to determine how far the ball has fallen.

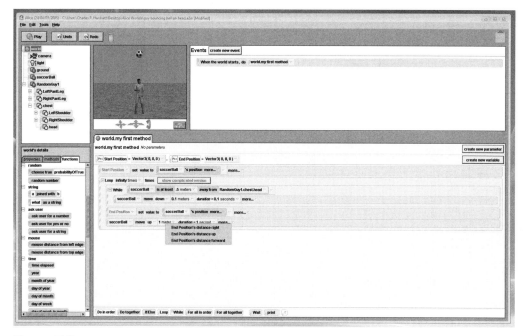

Figure 7.6
Saving the current position of the soccer ball.

The distance to move back to the start position is the End Position minus the Start Position.

13. Select the End Position in the Move Up command, and the pop-up menu options will appear, as shown in Figure 7.7. Select End Position Distance and then choose 1 as the value to subtract. Here again the 1 is just a placeholder.

14. Drag the Start Position variable over the 1 so that Start Position is now subtracted from End Position.

15. Click Play to see the result.

To test the difference, you can now move the ball farther up by clicking on it and dragging it up. Now it is more than 1 meter way from the guy's head. Click Play again, and see if it will still work. You have successfully worked with one example of basic collision detection. The next example shows you how to use another basic collision detection proximity function that determines whether an object is within the threshold space of another object and repels if it is.

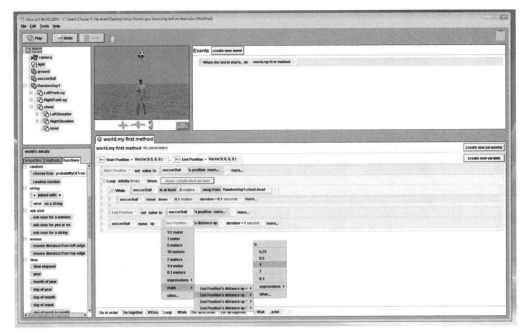

Figure 7.7
Changing the value of Move Up to be a formula based on the End Position and Start Position.

Alice Moving Around Furniture

It is common to have a virtual world that has objects that the users may need to navigate. For example, in a social network virtual world there are typically buildings and rooms in the buildings. You have to navigate the buildings, and when you enter a room you have to walk around the furniture in the room. Video games often have the same type of scenarios. Whether you are building a social network virtual world or a video game, you will probably find a need for this type of collision detection.

In this section, you will start with a simple scene with a character and a single object. Then you will learn how to efficiently handle more than one object. To get started, create a new world that contains just one character such as the Alice character and an object such as the Arm Chair object. Remember you must go into design mode to accomplish this setup with the objects in the Gallery. An example is shown in Figure 7.8; yours does not have to look the exact same as the one in this figure.

1. Create some events, as shown in Figure 7.9. You create such events by clicking the Create New Event button and selecting Let Arrow Keys Move *object* and When World Starts.

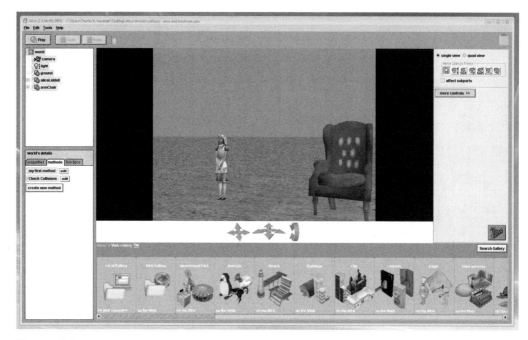

Figure 7.8
A simple virtual world with a character and an object for testing collision detection.

Figure 7.9
Events that are created for moving the character and for checking for collisions.

The first event will be used just to move the main character. The second event will be used to start collision detection. This should be its own event because you want the collision detection to always happen while you move the character around. So events are another activity in Alice that can happen simultaneously; the Do Together is the other.

2. Select the None for the new arrow keys event, and from the menu select the entire aliceLiddell object. This will assign the aliceLiddell object to the arrow keys to allow the users to move her around the world.

3. Select World from the object tree and select the Methods tab. Click the Create New Method button and name the new method **Check Collisions**. Then drag the method to the When World Starts event over the None. Your screen should look like Figure 7.9 when you have completed these tasks. The Check Collisions method determines whether your aliceLiddell object bumps into the chair object. This function can be used to check for collisions all over the virtual world between different objects. It will do this with the help of other methods.

4. Select the World object and then the Functions tab. Create a new function whose type is Boolean, and name the function **DetectCollision**. This function is one of those helper methods for Check Collisions. This function will determine if there is a collision between the aliceLiddell object and the chair. If you have other objects to compare, you can create another function for each pair of objects and put them all in the Check Collisions method. You are probably wondering about the Boolean. The Boolean is there because this function will either be True if there is a collision or False if there is no collision.

5. Figure 7.10 shows the body of the DetectCollision function. Start by dragging the IfElse into position.

6. Select the Alice character and then select the Functions tab. In the list of proximity functions, you will see one called Distance To. Drag it into place and set the values shown in Figure 7.10. The Distance To function determines how close you are to an object. If you are about to touch the object, in most cases this will result in a value that is less than 1. This works best for objects about the size of the chair and smaller. Now that this function is

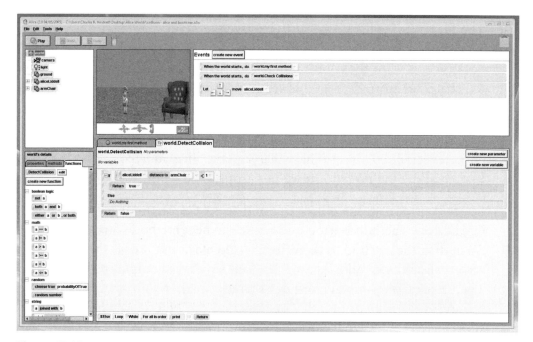

Figure 7.10
This shows the DetectCollision function.

complete, you should turn your attention to the Check Collisions method of the World object.

7. Select the World object in the object tree, and then select the Methods tab.

8. The Check Collisions method should be there from Step 3. Now click Edit next to the name of the Check Collisions method.

9. Fill in the body of this method by looking at Figure 7.11. First drag the Loop structure into place. Second, drag the IfElse structure into Loop body. Finally, drag the move for the aliceLiddell character into place. Remember to use Figure 7.11 to set the correct values and to compare your result.

10. Select the World object in the object tree, and drag and drop the Detect Collisions method over the True that would have been in your If statement condition (it is also possible that you chose to put False as the default condition).

    This loop is needed because as you move around the screen, the computer should always check for collisions. The event makes sure this method is

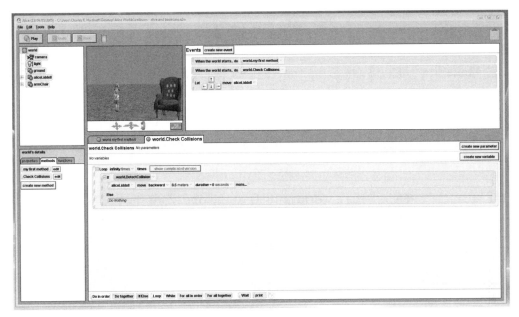

Figure 7.11
This figure shows the body of the Check Collisions method.

started when the world starts. The loop ensures that the program will never stop checking for collisions during the execution of the virtual world.

Notice how the IfElse statement uses your True/False (Boolean) function DetectCollision as a helper function. If the collision is detected, the Alice character backs up away from the object that she has just collided with.

You have completed another collision-detection scenario that includes the movement of a main character controlled by the user. You can use this method for characters that are programmed to move on their own. You can also extend this method to handle more than one object. This is what you will learn next.

Using Advanced Collision Detection

In a social network virtual world and a game, there are many objects that need to be checked for collision detections. For example, when a room has several pieces of furniture, all of these pieces of furniture need to be checked for collisions at all times. In this case, it is necessary to develop a way for handling all of these collision-detection checks. To solve this problem, you will use the following concepts:

- Make the collision-checking function more general so that it works with any obstacle.

- Use a list and parallel (simultaneous) execution to check all of the obstacles simultaneously. The list will contain all of the obstacles you want to check for collisions.

In Figure 7.12, you will see a world similar to the one from the previous exercise. It is easier to solve this problem using the result from the previous exercise. Therefore, if you have not completed previous section, I suggest that you finish that first.

If you have completed the previous section, use Save As… from the File menu and save it to another name. Then go to the design mode and add two more objects, such as the bookshelf and the table that have been added to the world in this example. Now use the following steps:

1. Return to the programming mode, and find the Detect Collision function within the World object. Click on Create New Parameter and name the parameter **An Obstacle**. The type of the obstacle should be Object.

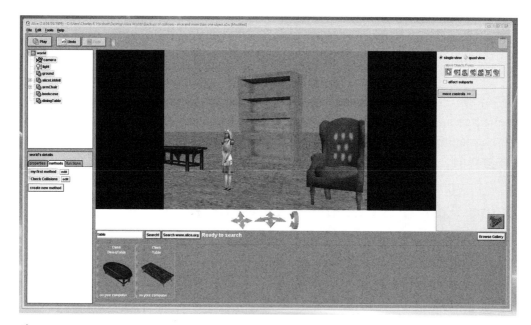

Figure 7.12
An example world with three obstacles placed in it.

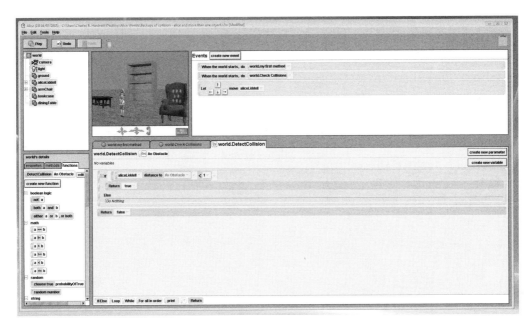

Figure 7.13
This shows the result after creating a parameter and replacing the arm chair reference.

2. Now, drag and drop the An Obstacle parameter over the Arm Chair reference in the IfElse condition. Your function should now look like Figure 7.13.

   This function will now work for any object that is passed to it when the function is called. You are now ready to change the call, which is in the Check Collisions method for World.

3. Select the Properties tab for the world and click Create New Variable. Name the new variable **All Obstacles**, as shown in Figure 7.14 (left). Next, select the Make List option. Finally, add the objects to the list that are obstacles for the world, as shown in Figure 7.14 (right).

   To make the method check all of the obstacles, you need to add a new loop and the list to the method.

4. Drag and drop the For All Together tile at the top of the loop before the IfElse statement. From the pop-up menu, select Expressions and then choose World.All Obstacles.

5. Drag and drop Item from All Obstacles from the For All Together feature to the If statement to replace None as the parameter of the DetectCollision function. This is how the function you modified is called with each of the objects in the scene. The result is shown in Figure 7.15.

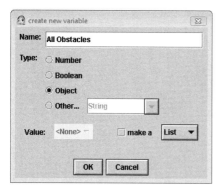

Figure 7.14
Creating a list of objects.

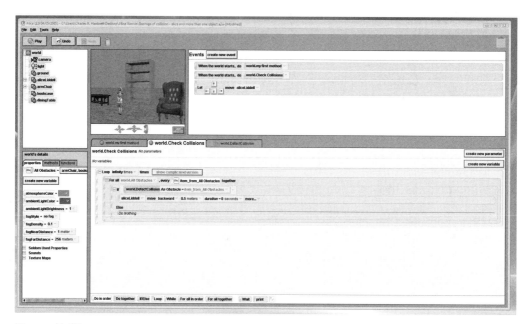

Figure 7.15
This figure shows the updated Check Collisions method that examines all obstacles.

It's important to note that the For All Together feature should work well in most cases. However, if you experience any slow-down in your game when you have a large number of objects in the scene, you may want to look at changing your collision detection to reduce the number of objects being checked.

6. Click the Play button and then move the character around the scene. Try bumping into objects, and voilá, it works.

The method used here generalizes the DetectCollision function to work for all obstacles. You can use this method to handle multiple characters as well. To do this, simply follow these steps:

1. Add a second parameter to the DetectCollision function for Any Character, and replace the reference to Alice with the new parameter.

2. Create a list of characters.

3. Add another For All Together in Check Collisions so that the current For All Together sits inside of the new one. The new one should use the list of characters.

In addition, you can add sound effects when a collision happens or update a score (scoring is covered in Chapter 10). You can even develop your own collision-detection functions using some of the other distance functions that find distance in front, distance behind, distance to the left, distance to the right, distance above, and distance below.

Summary

This chapter gave you an introduction to collision detection and covered some of the theoretical background. This introduction also explained how to use several *proximity* functions that are found in Alice. You learned some basic and some advanced collision-detection techniques. You may be wondering how to keep score based on catching a ball or touching something, and those ideas are explained in Chapter 10. Therefore, you will see other examples of collision detection. You also learned about some of the limitations of Alice's collision detection using proximity functions. It should be noted that this is a limitation in the Alice software that may not exist in other software for building virtual worlds and games. I encourage you to play with other techniques that can be used in the DetectCollision function and within the Check Collisions method that are interesting and/or more suitable to your needs. Remember, I am showing you an introduction, but you can learn even more by experimenting! I'll see you at the next chapter.

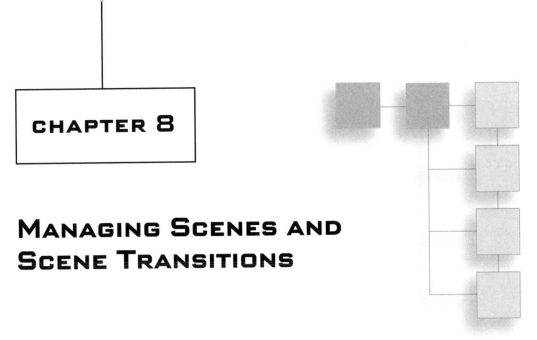

CHAPTER 8

MANAGING SCENES AND SCENE TRANSITIONS

A *scene* can be described as the place where the action happens in a story or movie. A movie is composed of several scenes. Each scene is an important part of the story. For example, consider your favorite movie. What is the opening scene? What is a scene in the middle of the movie? What is the scene at the end? One of my favorite movies is *Raiders of the Lost Ark*. This movie has many scenes as most movies do, but its scenes take place around the world. The first scene takes place in a jungle in South America. One of the middle scenes takes place in the city of Cairo, Egypt. Finally, the closing scene takes place in Washington, D.C. in a warehouse where stacks of thousands of "top-secret" crates are kept by the U.S. Government.

If you think about video games, you will see that even the simplest video games are composed of scenes as well. Sometimes there is one scene per level and other times there are numerous scenes per level.

In this chapter, you will be introduced to a few techniques that can help you manage scenes in Alice. The chapter covers the following objectives:

- Discuss the idea that underlies making scenes in the Alice world

- Show two methods for handling scene transitions

- Use invisible settings to move characters in and out of scenes

- Use dummy drops to indicate scenes

Creating Scenes in Alice

Alice is based on a virtual world. When you start the virtual world, it has a ground. It appears that the world is relatively endless. However, this is not the case at all. In fact, do you recall the time of Christopher Columbus and many of his contemporaries, who thought the world was flat? Of course, that is not something we believe now, but it's the truth for Alice. The Alice virtual worlds are flat!

Figure 8.1 shows a top-down view of an Alice world. As you can see from the figure, the ground in the Alice virtual world is flat, and you can also see that it's really a large square. You can place objects anywhere within the boundaries of the square/ground of the virtual world. You can use the fact that the world has boundaries to your advantage when you are creating scenes.

There are basically two methods you can use for managing scenes and they are actually based on stage plays and movies:

- **Stage Scene Method:** In this approach, there is a stationary stage and camera. At the start of a scene, the characters and props are placed into position. After the scene is over, the characters and props are removed from the scene.

- **Movie Scene Method:** In this approach, the virtual world is divided into several locations, and the camera and the characters move from one scene to

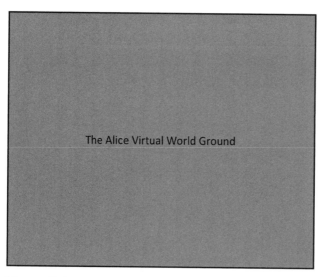

The Alice Virtual World Ground

Figure 8.1
This is a top-down view of an Alice virtual world.

the other. At the start of a scene, all characters and props are moved to the scene, and then the camera is moved to show the scene. At the end of the scene, the characters and props are moved out of the scene followed by the camera moving to the next scene.

These two approaches are the focus of the remainder of this chapter. You may decide to use one or both of these approaches in your virtual world projects. I will start with the stage scene method followed by the movie scene method.

Using the Stage Scene Method

The stage scene method is illustrated in Figure 8.2. In this illustration, you can see that there is an area designated as the stage. The stage is where you would set up your scenes. You would start with an opening scene setup using ideas shared in Chapter 4. However, you must also deal with scene changes using the stage as the scene. The camera is shown to have a field of view that is the entire stage. There are invisible boundaries for the stage, and you would typically define those for your world and maintain them throughout the running of the virtual world.

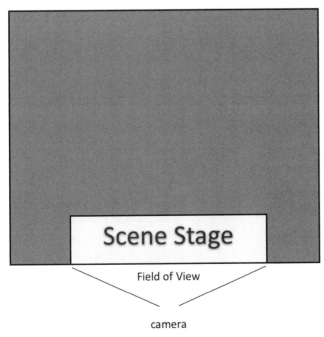

Figure 8.2
This figure shows a depiction of how the stage scene method is set up.

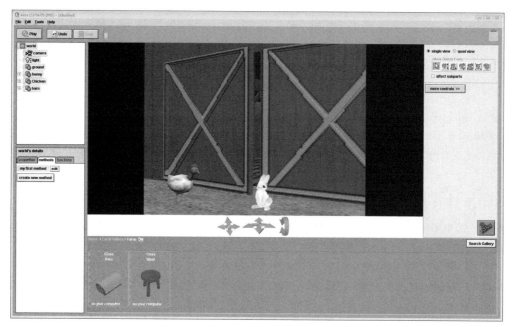

Figure 8.3
An opening scene with two animals and a barn.

How do you move objects on and off the stage? There are several ways you can do this. One approach is to dim the screen as if a curtain has fallen and then make your characters appear already in position as if they were just beamed into position. Let's explore this technique.

To start, create a new world and place two or three characters or other objects in the world. In Figure 8.3, the opening scene contains a bunny and a chicken with a barn in the background.

After you place the characters you want in your scene, go back to the programming mode and follow these steps:

1. Select the World from the object tree and then select the Methods tab in the details pane. Create a new method called **Show Scene1,** as shown in Figure 8.4.

2. Drag a Do Together tile into the program.

3. Select the Bunny object and then the Properties tab in the Details pane. You will drag the Is Showing property into the program and set it to False. This is shown in the Details pane, shown in Figure 8.5.

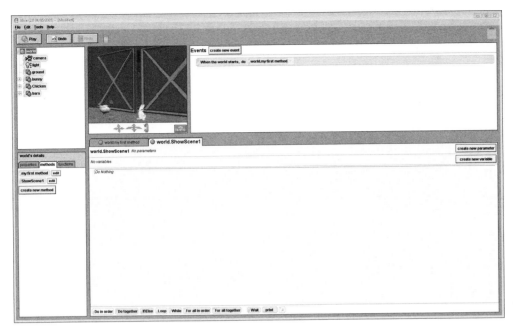

Figure 8.4
This figure shows the Worlds method called Show Scene1.

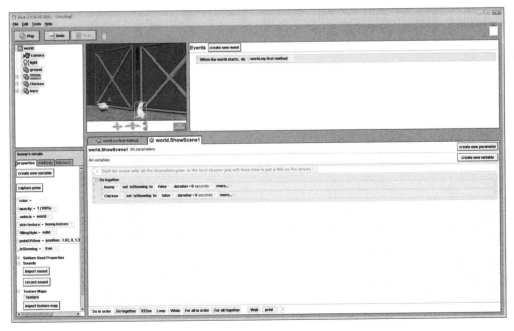

Figure 8.5
This figure shows how to make the characters invisible.

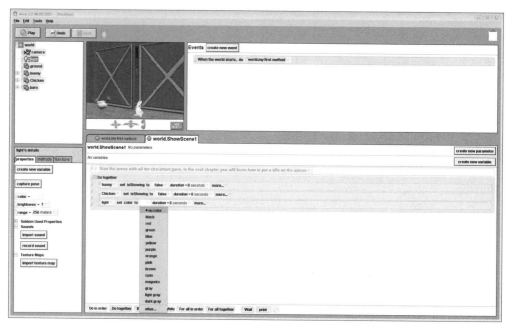

Figure 8.6
This figure shows how to dim the "stage lights" as if a curtain was being closed.

4. Select Light from the object tree and drag its Color property into the program, as shown in Figure 8.6. Select Black for the color.

   Notice how all of the commands execute within a Do Together with a duration of 0. This makes the scene appear to open instantaneously.

5. Use Figure 8.7 to complete the opening scene. The dramatic pause in this method is just there for later, when you will learn to add some title text to the scene. But it also allows you to see what is happening when you play the world. Changing the color of the light to ''no color'' and setting a duration of 2 raises the curtain. This provides a fade-in effect. You can alter the duration to make the effect the way you like it.

6. Select the My First Method tab and select World from the object tree. This is the method that starts up when the world starts. Drag the Show Scene1 method into this body of the My First Method. This is shown in Figure 8.8. Now click the Play button.

You have learned a very nice way to handle the opening of a scene. You can close the scene by following the same steps in reverse order. Make sure you create a new method in World before you do this. The result is shown in Figure 8.9.

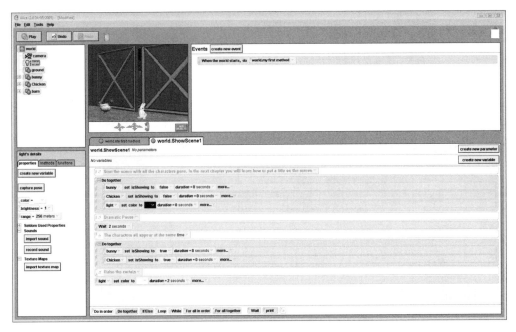

Figure 8.7
The completed opening scene method.

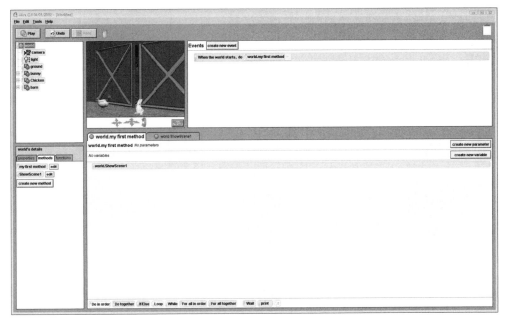

Figure 8.8
This figure shows how to open scene 1 from the first method.

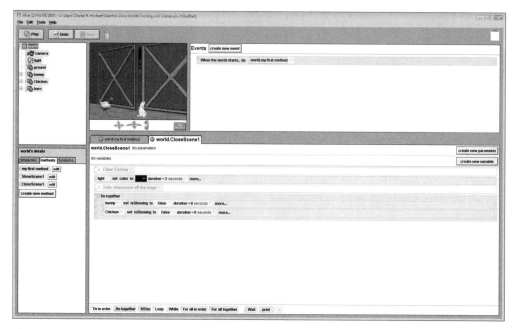

Figure 8.9
This figure shows the closing scene method.

The code shown in Figure 8.10 gives an example of how to use these scene functions and the transitions you have put into them. By creating methods for opening the scene, the performance, and closing the scene, you have more flexibility in using them, and you can add transitions. You should adopt this method-based style to make things easier to manage. This style of programming is called *modular programming*.

Although this is one way to get characters on and off the screen, there are many others. Students of mine have made their characters slide into the scenes from the left and right. Some have made them fly in from the top of the screen or emerge from underground. The idea behind all of these methods is to start with the characters out of the camera's view, and then use move commands to bring them into view. An example of the characters coming up from the ground is shown in Figure 8.11.

The program in Figure 8.11 is essentially the same Show Scene1, but instead of the characters being invisible, they are moved down below the ground. This puts them out of sight. I chose 5 meters because I knew that would be far enough down so that no part of them would be showing. Also, the duration should be 0

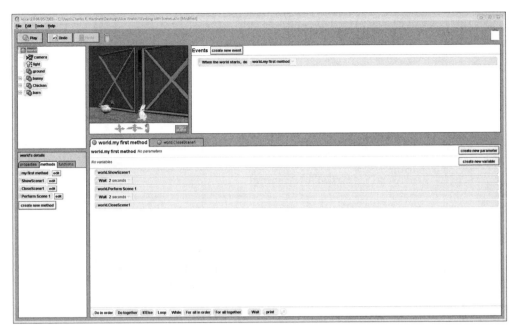

Figure 8.10
This figure shows the execution of the open scene and close scene in the first method.

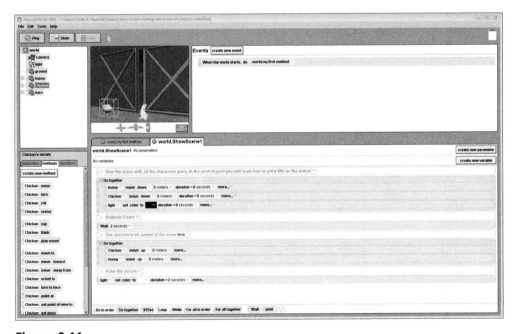

Figure 8.11
This shows another opening scene where the characters come up from the ground when the world is played.

for the moves down. However, moving up the duration is the default of 1 second. This is because you want to see the characters move up into the scene to give the dramatic effect. You can change the duration to alter this effect.

You should play with the techniques for stage effects and develop some of your own. In the next section, you will learn to move the camera in a movie-like way for your scenes.

Using the Movie Scene Method

The movie scene method mimics the approach used in films. With this method the scenery for the scenes and supporting characters may be prearranged in the scene or it can be programmed. The idea is that you focus on moving the camera to each scene. Each scene is located in different parts of the world. As you saw earlier, the Alice virtual worlds are actually flat and the ground is a square.

Figure 8.12 shows the Alice world subdivided into four quadrants. Each quadrant will be the home of a scene. These lines are imaginary lines, so do not expect to see them in Alice. However, they give you an idea of how this method works. You will write your virtual world program in such a way that you move the camera to these different areas. The camera is just like any other object in Alice and can be managed with the basic Alice methods.

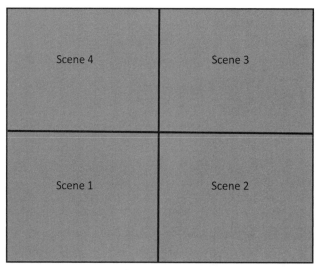

Figure 8.12
An example of subdividing the world into four scenes.

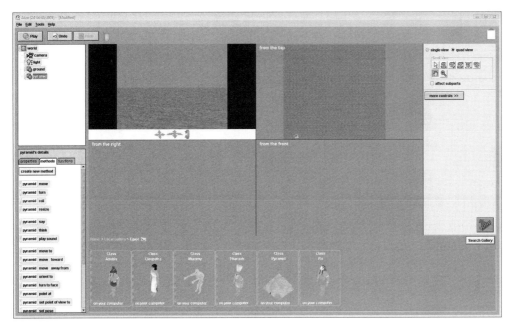

Figure 8.13
This figure shows the design mode in Quad-View so that you can see the entire world from the top.

To practice using this method, you need to create a new world and then go to the design mode, as shown in Figure 8.13. You will have to enter the Quad-View.

1. Click the magnifying glass, and select the ground in the top view. Move the mouse down while holding the mouse button. The ground should appear to get smaller. Do this until the entire ground is in the pane.

2. Now locate the Pyramid in the gallery and place it in the lower-left corner. To do this, you need to add and then select it in the object tree. You can then use the Move Objects Freely tool from the toolbox to click and drag the Pyramid object.

3. Use Figure 8.14 as a guide to place landmark objects in the other three scene areas:

    Lower-Right (Scene 2): Haunted House

    Upper-Right (Scene 3): Stadium

    Upper-Left (Scene 4): City Terrain

    These landmark objects become the focal point for the camera moves. The next few steps show you ways to position the camera so you get very good shots of the scenes.

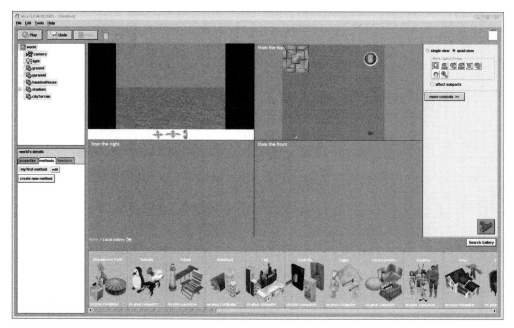

Figure 8.14
This shows the world with landmarks in the four scene areas.

4. In order to move the camera to each scene quickly in the design mode, you will use a method called Camera Get a Good Look At This. If you recall, you used this in an earlier situation to move the camera to look at some huskies in the midst of trees. Well, here you are again. The difference this time is that you want to adjust the camera position in each scene to get the best camera angle for your scene. The next few steps show you how to do different angles using each scene as an example. You should also consider trying some of your own ideas to get used to playing with the camera angles.

5. Right-click on the Pyramid object in the object tree and you should see a menu like the one in Figure 8.15. Select Camera Get a Good Look At This, which will move the camera to a pretty nice angle. However, it would be nice sometimes to move the camera more at ground level.

6. To fine-tune the camera position, you have to use the camera control arrows from the main world window. From left to right, the controls are:

Move camera left, right, up, and down.

Move camera pan right, pan left, zoom in, and zoom out. Pan is just the effect of the camera swiveling left and right.

Tilt camera forward and backward.

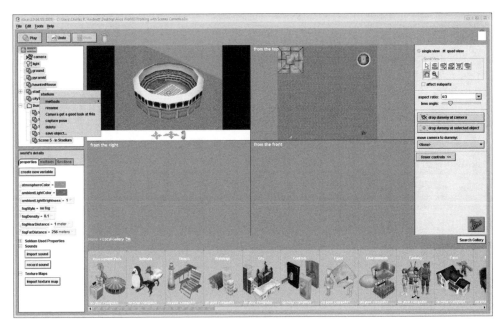

Figure 8.15
This shows how to move the camera quickly to a focus position where you can fine-tune it.

7. Select the camera in the object tree and then select the Properties tab. Focus on the position property while you hold down the Move Down camera control to move the camera down. The position starts with three values that represent the X, Y, and Z positions. You want to move down until the Y position reaches about 10.00.

8. Now select the Tilt Down arrow for the camera control and hold it until you get it where it looks like the camera is at ground level and the whole Pyramid is in view.

9. Once the camera is in place, you need to select the Drop Dummy at Camera button, as shown in Figure 8.16. This will make a dummy in the object tree. Rename the dummy object **Scene 1: Pyramid**. Figure 8.17 shows where the dummy objects will show up in the object tree.

10. To create the drop at scene number 2, you can right-click on the Haunted House in the object tree and select Camera Get a Good Look At This. The camera will move to the Haunted House object.

11. Use the camera controls to move the camera down until you have a good ground view of the Haunted House. You can use Steps 7 and 8 to help you with this movement.

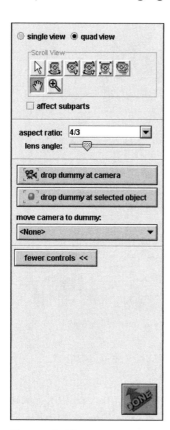

Figure 8.16
This shows the controls for dummy drops.

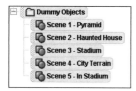

Figure 8.17
This shows the object tree of the completed dummy objects.

12. Now repeat Step 9 to create a dummy drop named **Scene 2: Haunted House**.

13. Scene 3 will be for the stadium. Here, you will create two dummy drops—one at the Camera Get a Good Look At This position (see Figure 8.18 (a)), and one inside the stadium (see Figure 8.18 (b)).

14. Right-click on the stadium and select Camera Get a Good Look At This. This should give you a view like Figure 8.18 (a). Drop a dummy object at this camera and call it **Scene 3: Stadium**.

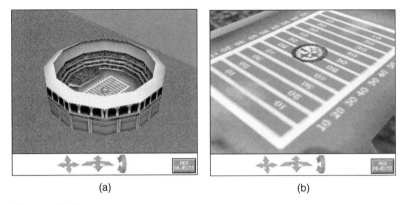

(a)   (b)

Figure 8.18
This shows the outside stadium view (a) and the inside stadium view (b).

15. Use the camera controls to zoom into the stadium (you may have to zoom in to the walls to keep going) and get a view similar to Figure 8.18 (b). Drop another dummy object here and call it **Scene 3: In Stadium**.

16. You can create scene 4 by using Camera Get a Good Look At This on the City Terrain object, and then dropping a dummy object at that camera location.

You have created five dummy drops now, and they should have names like those shown in Figure 8.17. Now it's time to create methods for your program to move you from one scene to another. The scene methods are useful because you can add special visual effects, sounds, text, and other features to customize your scene transitions.

1. Go back to program mode, and select the World.

2. Create new a new method called **GoToScene 1** (see Figure 8.19).

3. Click and drag the camera object from the object tree into the body of your new method. Select Set Point of View To from the Methods menu and then choose Scene 1: Pyramid from the Dummy Objects menu. The cascading menu is shown in Figure 8.19.

   Now you have a method to jump to Scene 1 that will give you the perspective that you created in the design mode for this scene. This is because the dummy object saved that location for you and the Set Point of View uses that dummy object as the target for moving the camera.

4. Create the other three methods according to the methods shown in Figure 8.20.

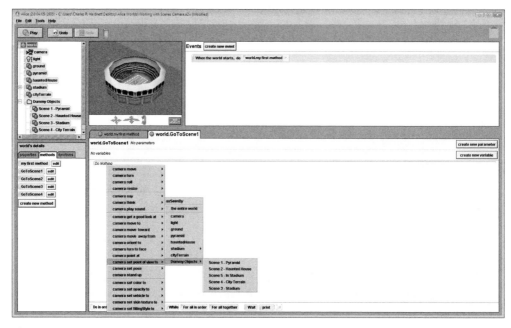

Figure 8.19
This shows the creation of GoToScene 1 using the camera Set Point of View To method.

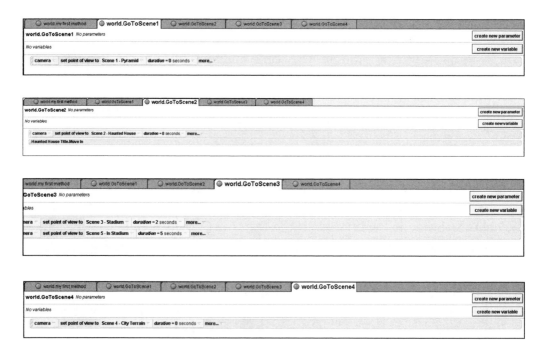

Figure 8.20
All of the methods for going to scenes 1 through 4.

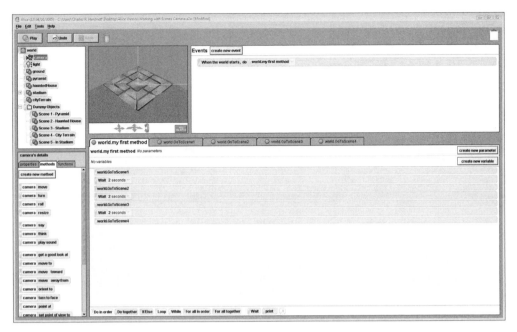

Figure 8.21
The first method calling all of the scene methods.

Each of the methods is similar. In some cases the duration is set to 0 and other cases it's some number of seconds like 2 or 5. The purpose of setting it to 0 is to get an instantaneous change in the camera position. This is like having no transition between scenes. However, the duration being set to 2 or 5 will give the perception that the camera is moving like a "fly-by" or is zooming in. This provides a different transition between scenes. Feel free to try other transitions in these methods, such as sounds or changes in the lighting.

It's time to see your results. Go to the My First Method method, and drag the Go To Scene methods so that you have a program like the one shown in Figure 8.21. Press the Play button to see your scene transitions.

Summary

In this chapter, you learned to handle scenes as if you were modeling your virtual world as a stage performance or as a movie. During these exercises, you learned how to manipulate the lighting, move the characters as they enter and leave scenes, and move the camera. You also continued to use the *modular program-ming* technique by assigning tasks to methods. The next chapter explores adding sound effects and dialogue to your world. As with other chapters, there are examples using the techniques of this chapter on the accompanying CD in the Chapter 8 folder. Good Luck!

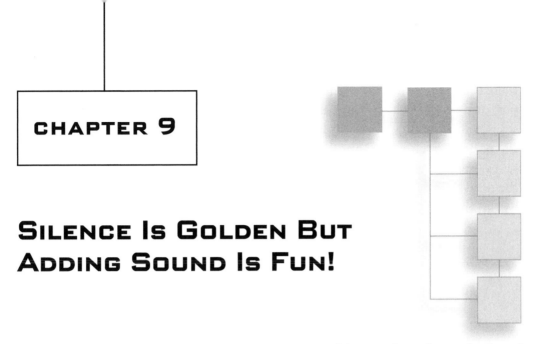

CHAPTER 9

SILENCE IS GOLDEN BUT ADDING SOUND IS FUN!

You have come a long way in creating virtual worlds. You have learned a lot of techniques that require a wide variety of skill. Some of the techniques are easy and others are more complex. In all cases, the examples and worlds you may have built are very quiet. Your worlds do not have any sound in them at all. Hearing is one of our six senses and whenever you want to engage a user in your virtual world, you have to appeal to as many senses as you can. Therefore, you need to learn to include sounds. These sounds can be anything ranging from sound effects, background music, speaking, and so on. In this chapter you will learn how to incorporate various types of sound elements into your virtual worlds.

Video games make use of many sounds. For example, a sports game such as *Madden Football* incorporates background music and sound effects for each button that is pressed when the player choosing options to set up the game. During the game, there is background noises that you would hear at a typical football game: cheers from the crowd, grunts by players, feet and bodies hitting the ground, shoulder pads clashing, the commentators calling the game, and maybe even airplanes flying overhead. These sounds add realism to the game for the players. These sounds can elicit emotions from the player. When you hear the crowds getting louder and some hard bass music playing it gets you pumped up to play the game harder, and you get more into the game.

Music and sound effects are not just limited to video games. Animated movies have the same elements: sound effects and background music. These sounds are there to help tell the story. The music may have an upbeat tempo if the current part of the story is happy and cheerful, or it may have a slow tempo and mellow sounds if there is currently sadness in the story. In addition, sound effects help the person watching the movie to become more captivated by the movie, and it helps them to mentally escape into the movie. And of course, you cannot forget the need to speaking dialogue. If you want to have some speaking in your virtual world, then this chapter can help you.

In this chapter you are expected to learn about the following concepts:

- Where to find sound effects and how to obtain them

- How to add sound effects and music to your Alice worlds

- How to create your own sounds including recorded speech

I hope you enjoy this chapter, and as always allow this chapter to serve as an introduction to the possibilities. You need to take the ideas of this chapter and match them with those of other chapters for creative solutions when creating your own virtual worlds.

Where Are Sound Effects?

Sound effects can be found at several websites online. You can either download the sounds from the website or you can purchase a CD that contains several. A sound effect is a file like an MP3 file or WAV file or any other music file format. In turns out that making and distributing sound effects is pretty good business for many and so you will come across several places where there is a fee to download the effects or CDs.

In this section, I will show you some places to get sound effects for free because they are copyrighted in the public domain. Below is a list of sites that I have used and some of my students have used:

- Partners in Rhyme (http://www.partnersinrhyme.com/pir/PIRsfx.shtml)

- The Free Site (http://www.thefreesite.com/Free_Sounds/Free_WAVs/)

- Stonewashed (http://stonewashed.net/sfx.html)

There are others, but these are some that I have had success with in the past. On these sites you will find various sound files and in various formats. The format of a sound file is just the way in which the sound is digitally encoded. Some encodings are for compression purposes to keep the file sizes small, and other encodings are meant to create higher quality sounds. In either case, there are two types of encoding formats that work well with Alice: WAV and MP3. WAV file formats have been the most reliable for the work I have done and what my students have done. So, you will probably have the most luck using WAV files. There are applications such as Audacity (http://audacity.sourceforge.net/) that can be useful for converting files from one format to the other. Audacity is freely available online and it works very well. There are instructions online on how to use it.

Downloading Sound Effects

The Partners in Rhyme is my favorite site. I like the way they have it organized and so I will be referring to that site as I explain these ideas. Their website is divided into the Free and the Commercial sounds. The free sounds are divided into categories such as:

- Ambient Sound Effects: Background sounds like nature or city sounds

- Vehicle Sound Effects: Airplanes, cars, or motorcycles

- Human Sound Effects: Laughter, applause, or sports sounds

- Animal Sound Effects: Dogs, cats, or bears

There are many other categories, but they help you locate the sounds you're looking for to enhance your virtual world.

Downloading sound effects is relatively simple. The problem is organizing them once you download them. I suggest creating a folder for each virtual world project that you are working on. You can then create subfolders for each scene. This way you know which sound file goes with a scene. If a sound effect is in more than one scene, then use file shortcuts. (See your Windows XP or Vista help to learn more about shortcuts.) It's time to download some sound effects:

1. Open your web browser and go to the Partners in Rhyme website (www.partnersinrhyme.com), as shown in Figure 9.1.

2. Click on the Airplanes and Helicopters, which is under the Vehicle Sound Effects heading (note that this is a website and subject to change). Then, choose the 707. In most browsers, the sound will then start to play.

3. In Figure 9.1, you can see where there is a link called Download This Sound Effect. Do not just click on the link. This will usually just download the file

Figure 9.1
This shows the browser window where the download of the sound takes place.

to a location that may be hard to find. Instead, right-click on the link and choose Save File As . . . from the pop-up menu.

4. You can now use the Save File As . . . dialog box to find your sounds folder and you can rename the file to a name that makes sense to you. I renamed my file airplane.wav. You must keep the .wav file extensions on these files.

That's it! You have successfully downloaded a sound effect. The key to downloading these files is to right-click on the link to access the pop-up menu. That way, you can save the file with your own name and in your chosen destination.

Adding Sound Effects to Your Virtual World

It's fun to listen to sound effects and download them to your computer, but it's even more fun to put those sound effects into your virtual world. That is what you are about to do. There are two examples in this section. The first example is of an airplane flying towards the camera. The second example associates a bunny hopping and a "whoo hoo" sound with the players pressing the spacebar.

To get started you must create a new world and add the Jet object to the world. Use the Quad-View in design mode to move the airplane far from the camera, and use the Jet object's Point Toward Camera Method to turn the plane toward the camera.

Associating Sounds with Alice Objects

You can associate sounds with any of the Alice objects. In Figure 9.2, the airplane.wav file is associated with the Jet object. Here are the steps to make that happen:

1. Select Jet from the object tree and then select the Properties tab from the Details pane.

2. Click the Import Sounds button and use the dialog box to find the folder where you saved the airplane.wav file.

3. Once the file is loaded, you can test it by clicking the green triangle next to the filename.

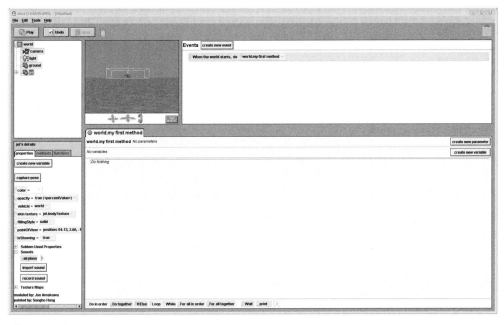

Figure 9.2
This figure shows the Airplane sound loaded into the Jet object.

Figure 9.3
This shows the construction of the fly-by code.

4. Use Figure 9.3 as the guide. The Play Sound method is brought in from the Jet object. Here you select the sound to play, which is jet.airplane in this case, because you imported the airplane sound into the Jet object.

5. Change the duration of the move to equal 9.671 (the length of the sound effect). Change the distance to move to 300 meters. This will make the sound play while the plane is in flight.

6. Click Play. Figure 9.4 shows the complete fly-by program. Check your program against this one if something is not working as planned.

This example shows the typical use of Do Together with the sound and the movement to make it natural. If you do not do this, the sound will play before or after the move, but not with it.

Associating Sounds Interactively

The second example is an interactive one. The entire program is shown in Figure 9.5. The Bunny object was added to the world. Next, the Jump method was added to the Bunny object.

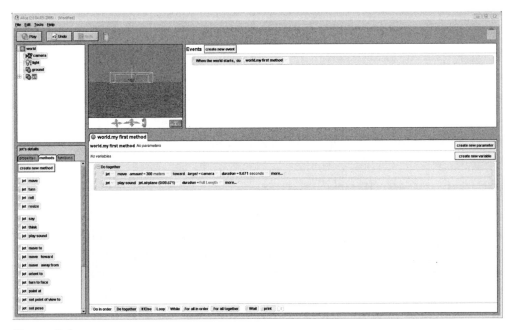

Figure 9.4
The complete fly-by code.

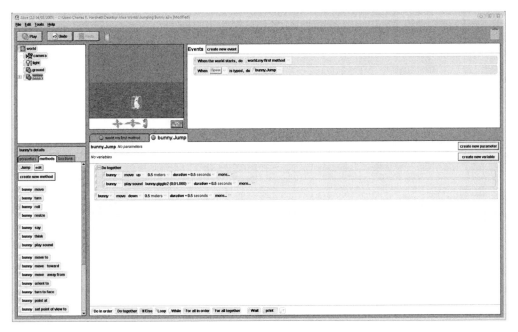

Figure 9.5
This figure shows an interactive example with sound effects.

The sound that was used here is found on the Partners in Rhyme website under Human Sounds. The name of the sound is Giggle. You can use any sound you want if you cannot find Giggle or if you just want something different. Download the sound and then import the sound into the Bunny object.

The details for the Jump method are shown in Figure 9.5. After you have replicated this method as shown in the figure, click Play. Each time you press the spacebar the bunny will jump and make a sound!

Adding Background Sounds

Background sounds can be music and/or different ambient noises. Background sounds should be controlled by an event. This is because events allow one method to execute while other methods are executing. This is called *parallelism*: the act of having two or more programming units executing at the same time. In this section, you will build the program shown in Figure 9.6.

I used the summer.wav file from the Nature Sounds section on the website. After you have downloaded this file, you can follow these steps to create the program:

1. The method BackgroundSounds is created as a part of the World methods.

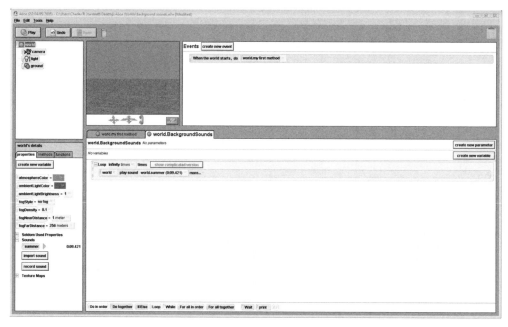

Figure 9.6
This figure shows the creation of a method for playing background sounds.

2. Drag the Loop tile into the method and choose "infinity" times for the number of iterations.

3. Drag the Sound tile from the Properties tab. This is another way to get the Play Sound method.

   The loop in this case will make the sound continue to play by *looping* the sound. This is a common technique where you have a short amount of sound that you need to play over a long period of time. When the sound reaches its end, it will just start from the beginning. Most sounds will not be perfect loops and so you will hear a small gap. However, most people don't hear it while they are focusing on the story or the game. If you want to remove the gap, you can edit the sound file using a program such as Audacity.

4. Create a new event using When the World Starts.

5. Drag the BackgroundSounds method to the event, as shown in Figure 9.7.

Now you will hear the sound continuously playing when you click the Play button.

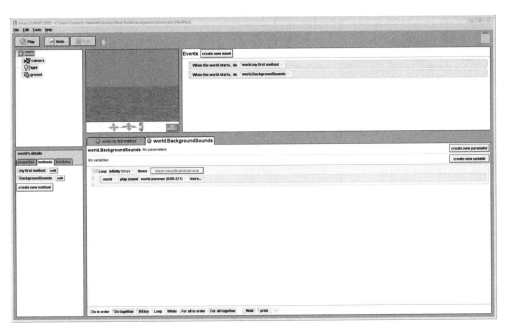

Figure 9.7
This shows how to get the background sound to play when the world starts.

Recording Your Own Sounds

Recording your sounds can be very helpful, especially if you want your characters to speak. You may also be interested in creating your own sound effects. In this section, I will explain how easy it is to record your own sounds.

There are two ways to record your own sounds. The first way is to use third-party software such as Audacity to record and save the dialogue as a .wav file. Programs like Audacity have the ability not only to record sounds from the microphone, but they also allow you to edit the sound (maybe to make it sound better or add something like an echo effect).

The second way to add your own sounds is to record the sounds directly into Alice. Recording into Alice directly is a very simple way to record; you cannot edit or enhances these recordings. However, in most cases, this approach is sufficient.

To get started, create a new world and add the Cow object to the world. Then go to the programming mode and follow these steps:

1. Select the Cow object in the object tree and then select the Properties tab. At the bottom there will be the Import Sound and Record Sound buttons, as shown in Figure 9.8.

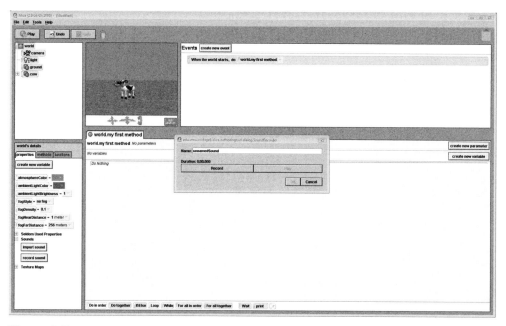

Figure 9.8
This figure shows what happens when the Record Sound button is pressed.

2. After clicking the Record Sound button, the dialog box shown in Figure 9.8 will appear.

3. Provide a name for the sound. I used "Hello, Welcome to Alice" as the name.

4. When you are ready to speak into the microphone, click the Record button. (The Record button changes to a Stop button once recording begins.)

5. Speak clearly into the microphone and your voice will be recorded. Click Stop button when you are done speaking. At this time, you can click Play to hear the recording or Record to overwrite it.

6. Click OK to save the sound.

I recorded myself saying "Hello, welcome to Alice". I also put the same text into the speech bubble. The sound and the speech bubble are in the Do Together, as shown in Figure 9.9. The duration of the speech bubble is slightly longer than the speaking sounds. This ensures that the spoken words are completely done before the bubble goes away. Once you click Play, voilá! The cow is talking!!

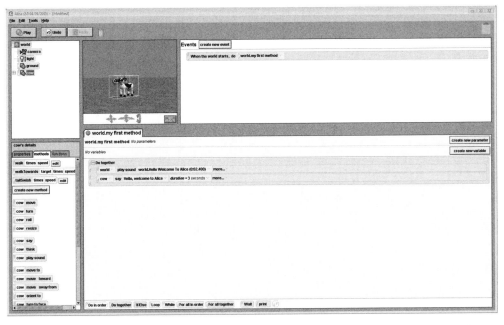

Figure 9.9
This figure shows the program with the cow speaking.

Summary

This chapter explores sounds via sound effects, background sounds, and spoken dialogue. As I said in the beginning, working with sounds is straightforward in Alice and it's a lot of fun! I hope that you start to implement these ideas in your own worlds and I hope that you are willing to experiment with the options and settings. Don't be afraid to combine different methods and create new effects.

CHAPTER 10

KEEPING SCORE: WINNERS AND LOSERS

If you have followed this book to build your own game or social network virtual world, you have learned how to design your project, control characters, animate characters, create scenes, add sound, determine when collisions have happened, and the list goes on. It's now time to look at how you can keep score to determine how well a player plays or to determine who wins and who loses.

You might be thinking that scoring is not necessary in a social network virtual world, but you would be incorrect. Scoring in a social network virtual world is not used for determining who wins, but it is used to determine what your character can purchase, or where your character is allowed to go in the world. For example, in social network virtual worlds such as *Second Life*, there is a virtual currency called a *Linden dollar* and it has a symbol L\$. As your avatar collects more L\$, your avatar can make purchases of goods and services. This is just like in real life, where if you earn money you can exchange your money for food, clothes, Internet service, cell phone service, and many other examples.

In this chapter, you will learn about the following:

- Design and implementation issues related to adding scoring mechanisms

- A basic scoring concept that is used in most projects

- A timer concept that can be used to count down time in your project

Background for Scoring

The scores for a game or social network virtual world are fairly straightforward to create. There are a few ideas that you should be aware of and these may influence how you implement scoring in your projects.

In most projects, the world object can manage the scores. This makes it easier to manage the scoring and to have access to the scores in any method and function. You will maintain the value of a score using a variable with a number type. You will need to set the score to its starting value at the start of your game or social networked world. This ensures that the score will always have the correct value. Remember that the "score" information is not only points earned by the player, but it can also be considered the number of lives the player has remaining or the time left in the game.

There are some projects where the score should not be maintained by the world. These are projects where more than one player is controlled by humans and/or computers. From a programming point of view, managing all of these scores and status information could prove to be difficult. Therefore, you need to keep track of the scoring with each character instead of with the world.

Finally, it is sometimes appropriate to mix the ideas. In a mixed or hybrid concept, you will have some scoring data maintained by the world and other scoring data maintained by the player's character. For example, consider a game such as basketball, where you need to keep the score for each team. These scores would probably be managed by the world. However, the points, rebounds, and other stats for each player are managed by each player's character.

Manipulating 3D Text

The score is typically going to be displayed using the 3D Text object. In this section, you learn how to update the contents of a 3D Text object. This first example uses mouse clicks to determine whether the score should increase or decrease. Figure 10.1 shows the initial scene for this world. You need to be in design mode, and start by adding the Chicken and Cow objects from the Object Gallery (see Chapter 4 if you do not remember how to do this). The new object is the 3D Text object:

1. Scroll through to the end of the gallery (the far right). Click on the 3D Text object.

2. In the dialog box, simply place a zero there. What you put in the dialog box is what actually appears on the screen.

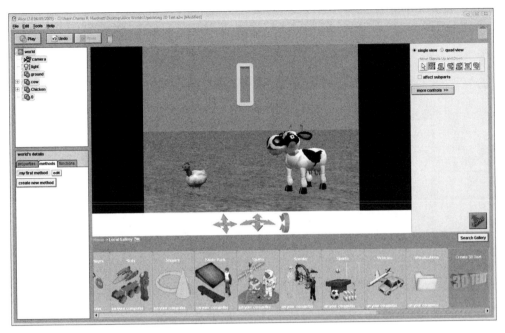

Figure 10.1
This figure shows the simple world with two characters and a score value.

After you have completed the setup of the initial screen, follow these steps to create the program:

1. Click on the Create New Event button and select the option When the Mouse Is Clicked On Something. Add two of these events, as shown in Figure 10.2.

2. Select the World object from the object tree and then select the Methods tab. Create two new methods called **Increment Score** and **Decrement Score.**

3. Select the Properties tab in the Details pane and click the Create New Variable to be called **Score Value.** Set its initial value to 0.

4. Drag and drop the Score Value variable into the body of the Increment Score method and select Increment by 1 from the pop-up menu. See Figure 10.3.

5. Select the 0 object from the object tree and choose its Properties tab.

6. Drag and drop the Text property into the body of the Increment Score method and choose Default String from the pop-up menu.

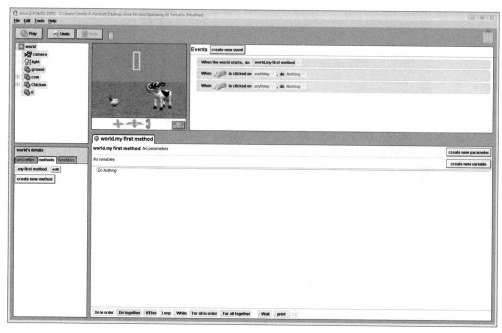

Figure 10.2
This shows the addition of two events for handling clicks.

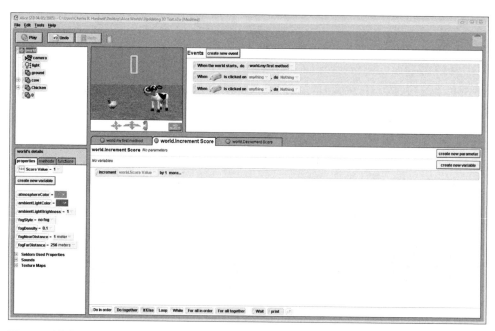

Figure 10.3
This shows the first part of the Increment Score method.

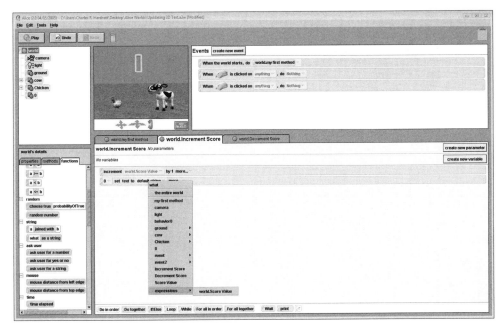

Figure 10.4
Shows the pop-up menu for the What As A String function.

7. Select the World object from the object tree and select its Functions tab from the Details pane.

8. Scroll to find the What As A String function and drag and drop it over the Default String in the 0 Set Text To command. The pop-up menu in Figure 10.4 is shown, and you should select Expressions and the World. Score Value.

    The completed Increment Score method is shown in Figure 10.5. This method now will increment the numeric variable Score Value and then convert that value to a string and place it in the 0 text object, which is the 3D text object that represents the score on the screen.

9. Select the Decrement Score method tab in the programming area.

10. Complete the Decrement Score method using the Steps 4-8 as you did for the Increment Score method. See Figure 10.6.

11. Go back to the Events pane and select Anything from the first mouse event and choose Cow and Entire Cow. Then select Nothing and choose World.Increment Score.

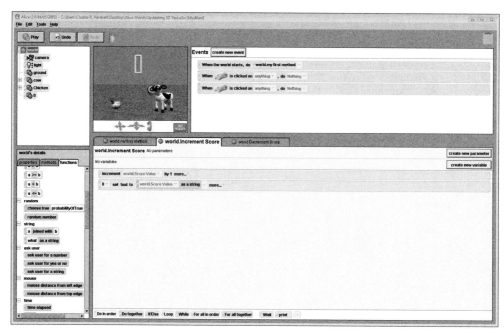

Figure 10.5
The completed Increment Score method.

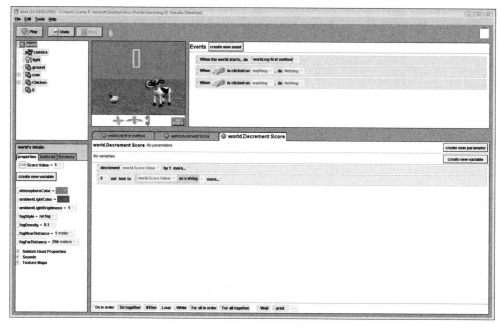

Figure 10.6
The complete Decrement Score method.

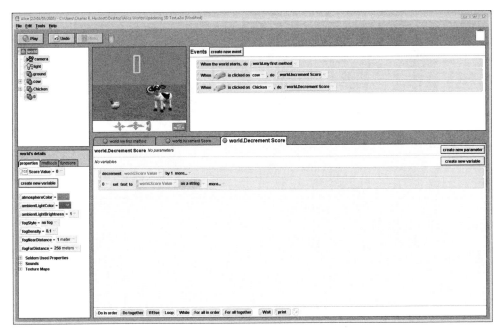

Figure 10.7
This figure shows the completed mouse click events.

12. Do the same for the second mouse event using the Chicken object and the World.Decrement Score method.

13. Click Play and click on the characters to make the score change. Figure 10.7 shows the completed mouse click events.

This example shows the basics for manipulating the 3D text object to change its displayed text dynamically. This technique is the core to handling score and status information that changes throughout the execution of your virtual world project. In the next section, you will use this technique as a part of a game.

Keeping Score In a Game

In this section, you will learn a basic scoring method that manages the score via the world. In order to provide a meaningful example for scoring, it is necessary to build a game of some sort that is simple and easy to understand. Therefore, you will not only learn some issues regarding scoring, but you will also have a refresher of issues covered in earlier chapters.

You should use Figure 10.8 as your guide. In this figure, you can see that you need to add a baseball glove and baseball to the world. The trick to this exercise is

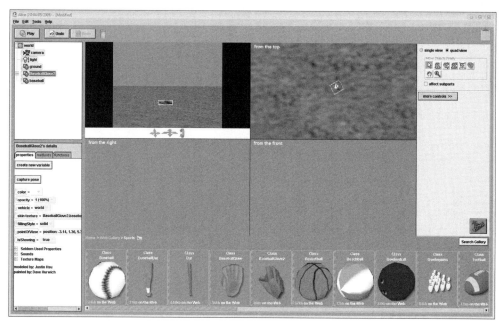

Figure 10.8
This shows how the world needs to be set to create this example.

that you need to get the ball aligned with the glove in the top view, as shown in Figure 10.8, and you need to allow the ball to be off the screen when using the normal camera angle.

The next part to create is a score in the lower-left corner of the screen. To do this, you go to the end of the local gallery and choose 3D Text. Add the text **Score** and position it in the lower-left corner. Right-click on the text, choose the method Turn to Face, and then choose Camera. Then do the same thing and add the text **0** to the right of the word Score. This is done as two parts because you need to write code to update the 0 to other numeric values as the game is played.

Once you have completed this, and your world looks like the one shown in Figure 10.9, you can go back to the programming mode and follow the steps:

1. Create two methods for the Baseball object. Name these methods **Position Ball** and **Drop Ball**. Select the tab for the Position Ball method.

   These methods are responsible for determining where the ball will drop down on the screen, and for animating the ball dropping down.

2. Click on the Properties tab and click the Create New Variable button. Create a new variable named **Start Position** of type Position.

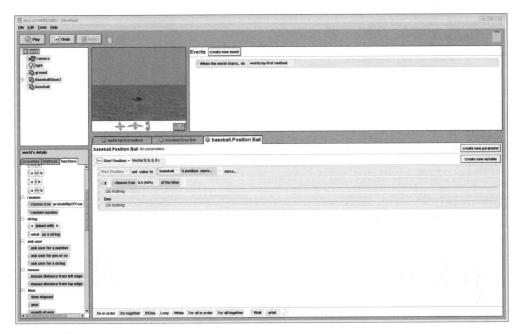

Figure 10.9
This shows the body of the ball positioning method.

3. Drag and drop the variable into the programming area for the Position Ball method. It will then create the Set Value To command, and you can set it to the default vector. This is a placeholder for the Baseball's position. This was done with the bouncing soccer ball on the guy's head in Chapter 7.

4. Select the Baseball object and then the Functions tab in the Details pane. Drag the function Baseball's Position to the vector to set the Start Position variable. This will set the Start Position to the current position of the baseball.

5. Drag and drop the IfElse tile and then use the functions from the World object to choose True some percentage of time. I am using 50% in this example.

   This function allows you to program Alice to randomly choose True or False. The value 50% is how you stipulate that Alice may choose True or False equally, like flipping a coin. If you use 30%, Alice will choose True 30% of the time and 70% of the time it will choose False. This is a rather nifty function. In this case, I am using it to determine the positioning of the ball. You will see how that develops in the next step.

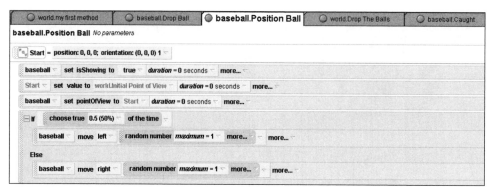

Figure 10.10
This shows the completed Position Ball method.

6. Use Figure 10.10 to complete the Position Ball method by adding the two Move operations.

Figure 10.10 shows that the IfElse is used to determine if the ball is moved to left of center or to the right of center. This increases the difficulty for the users trying to catch the ball because they will not know the starting position of the ball.

The next method is the Drop Ball method that animates the ball falling. This is done with one Move command just like it was done Chapter 7 with the soccer ball dropping on the guy's head.

7. Click on the Baseball object from the object tree and then click on its Methods tab.

8. Drag the Move command to the body of the Drop Ball method and set the parameters as shown in Figure 10.11.

9. Use Figure 10.12 to create the body of My First Method using the following steps:

A. Select the World object and then under the Properties tab, create a new variable called **The Score**. This variable will hold the value of the score in the game to be incremented and displayed.

B. In the Properties tab, set The Score to 0. This will initialize the score.

C. Click Create New Variable in the Properties tab and call this variable **Initial Point of View**. It is a Position type variable.

D. Drag and drop the variable into the body and set it to Default position.

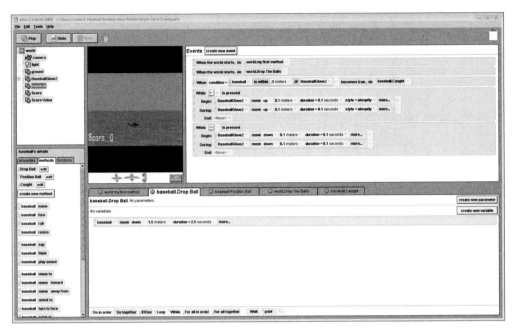

Figure 10.11
This is the Drop Ball method.

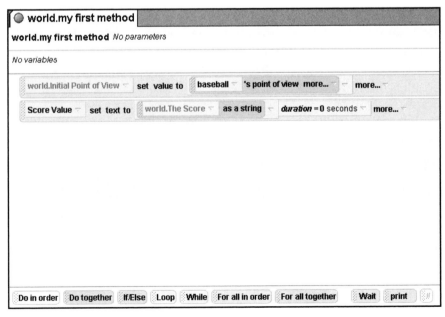

Figure 10.12
This shows the first method body.

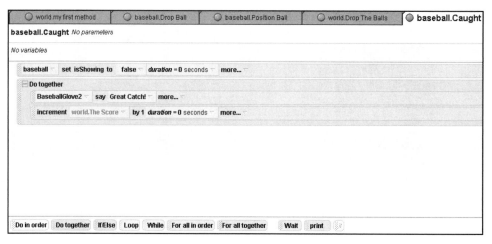

Figure 10.13
This figure shows the Caught method.

E. Select the Baseball object from the object tree, and then choose its Functions tab from the Details pane.

F. Drag and drop the Point of View function over the Default position. Once you have completed these steps, you should have a method that resembles Figure 10.12.

10. Figure 10.13 shows the body of the Caught method. This method is called if a collision between the ball and the glove is detected. It increments the Score variable that is a part of the World object. Follow these steps to create this method:

A. Select the Baseball object from the object tree and select the properties of the object in the Details pane.

B. Scroll down to find the Is Showing attribute, and drag and drop the attribute into the body of the Caught method. Set it to False. This allows the baseball to be hidden when it's caught as if it has disappeared into the glove.

C. Drag and drop a Do Together tile into the body. This structure allows you to have congratulatory message displayed at the same time the score is displayed.

D. Select the Baseball Glove object and drag its Say method into the Do Together tile. Set it to **Great Catch!**

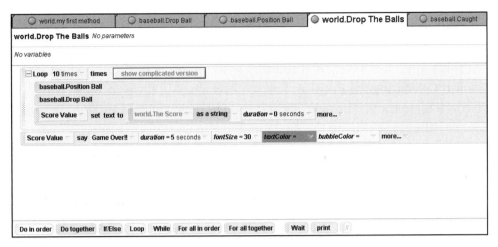

Figure 10.14
This shows the Drop The Balls method.

E. Select the World object and the Properties tab in the Details pane.

F. Drag the Score variable into the Do Together tile and select the Increment By 1 from the pop-up menu.

Once you have completed these steps, you will have a method that will react when the ball is caught in the glove.

11. Figure 10.14 shows the Drop The Balls method that can be used for completing this project. This method ensures that the game drops 10 balls at random positions. The position variables are used to make sure that each ball is dropped from the same location off-screen.

12. This method is also where the numeric score value is converted to string type so that it could be assigned the 3D Text object. The following steps build this method:

A. Select the World object from the object tree and then choose the Methods tab of the Details pane. Edit the Drop The Balls method.

B. Drag and drop the Loop tile into the body of the Drop The Balls method and set it to execute 10 times.

C. Select the Baseball object from the object tree and select the Methods tab of the Details pane. There will be two methods there: Position Ball and Drop Ball. These two methods are used by the Drop The Balls method you are building now.

D. Drag the Position Ball and Drop Ball methods into the body of the loop in the Drop the Balls method.

13. At this point, you have a method that will randomly position each of the 10 balls by executing the Position Ball method and will drop each ball using the Drop Ball method. The next set of steps will have you adding the support to display the score during the game and at the end of the game.

A. Select the Score Value object from the object tree and then select its Properties.

B. Drag and drop the Set Text attribute to the loop tile and select a default value such as 1. Figure 10.14 shows the Set Text attribute placed after the two method calls, but within the loop. It must be in the loop because you want the score to be displayed after each ball has been dropped.

C. Select the World object from the object tree and select the Functions tab from the Details pane.

D. Scroll and find the function called What As A string and drag and drop this function to the current value being set to Score Value (1). From the pop-up menu, select the World.The Score.

This step will change the numeric score value into a string value, which is a value that can be printed on the screen as output.

Whew! All of the functions are now completed; now you can turn your attention to the events. The events will bring all of the functions together so that the game can respond appropriately at the correct times. Use the following steps to construct the events for this game:

1. In Figure 10.15, there is a second event for When The World Starts that you need to create. The steps for creating this event are as follows:

A. Click on the Create New Event button and select When the World Starts from the menu.

B. Select the World object from the object tree and select the Methods tab from the Details pane.

C. Drag and drop the Drop The Balls method to None for this new event.

2. Using Figure 10.15, create a collision-detection event that starts when a condition is met. This event will have an expression to determine whether or not the ball hits the glove.

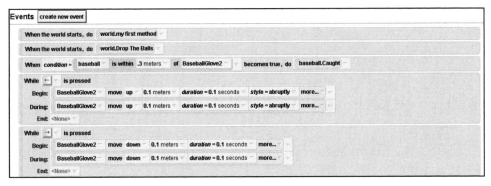

Figure 10.15
This figure shows the set of events that needs to be created.

    A. Click Create New Event and select the When Something Is True option.

    B. Select the Baseball object from the object tree and then select the Functions tab from the Details pane.

    C. Drag and drop the Within Threshold of Object function to True. Use the pop-up menu to select the options, as shown in Figure 10.15.

3. Also in Figure 10.15, there are events for moving left and right. To create the moving-left event, do the following:

    A. Click on the Create New Event button and select When a Key Is Pressed from the menu.

    B. Right-click on the new event and select Change To. Change the event to While instead of When.

    C. Select the Key parameter in the event and, from the menu, select Left Arrow.

    D. Select BaseballGlove from the object tree and Methods from the Details pane.

    E. Drag and drop the Move Up method to the Begin and During parts of the event. Set the parameters of the method to those shown in Figure 10.15.

You have to use Move Up to move to the left because the glove is lying on its side and the top (moving up) of the glove is pointing to the left. This is where you use the information you learned in the introduction to the 3D objects.

4. In Figure 10.15, there is another event for moving to the right. This event is very similar to the event that moves to the left.

A. Perform Steps 3 A and B again to create another While event for another key.

B. Select the Key parameter in the event and, from the menu, select Right Arrow.

C. Select the BaseballGlove from the object tree and then choose Methods from the Details pane.

D. Drag and drop the Move Down method to the Begin and During parts of this event. Set its parameters according to those in Figure 10.15.

Just as with the left movement, the moving down is in relationship to the new orientation of the glove. The bottom of the glove is pointing to the right.

5. Your scoring game is now complete. Click Play and you will see how well you can catch the balls. Good luck!

Setting a Timer

Game timers are very useful in many situations. You will usually find a game timer in situations where the game needs to let the users know their game time is running out and it can influence the strategy of the players. For example, in professional basketball teams had to develop new strategies when the shot clock was introduced. Before the shot clock, teams could keep passing and dribbling the ball when they had the lead to keep the other team from getting the ball and to run the game clock down. The shot clock puts a limit on the amount of time the team has to take a shot, which provides an opportunity for them to lose possession of the ball.

With the advent of the shot clock, teams could not use the strategy of holding the ball to maintain a lead; instead, the teams had to develop strategies that involved slowing down the game and creating opportunities to add to their lead by scoring. The same effect can be seen in games, when players have a time limit they have to sharpen or change their strategy to get the maximum number of points within the time limit. Timers found in games are usually countdown timers that start at some value greater than 0 and count down to 0. There are also timers that start at 0 and increment over time. The choice is yours, but the techniques are essentially the same.

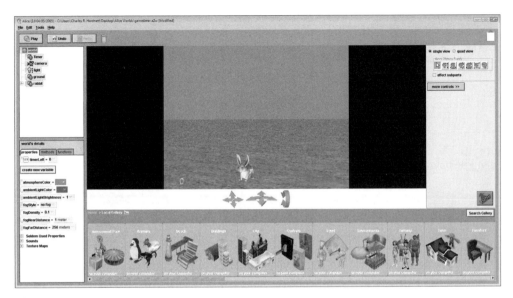

Figure 10.16
This is the design for the timer-based exercise.

In this section, you will be introduced to a method for creating your own timer. To complete this exercise, you need to create a simple world with a 3D text object that has the value of 0 and call it **Timer**. Also add a bunny character from the gallery. Your project design window should resemble what is shown in Figure 10.16.

The next few steps lead you to developing a timer that counts while the bunny hops. First is to set up the methods to support the timer. These three methods are created to manage the timer:

- **Timer Initialize:** Used to initialize the timer to some number of seconds.

- **Timer Countdown:** Used to decrement the counter and check that it has not reached 0.

- **Play Game:** Used as a placeholder for the start of the game or virtual world social networking.

These steps show you how to develop this project:

1. Select the World object from the object tree and select the Methods tab. Use the Create New Method to create the three methods described in the previous list.

Figure 10.17
The Timer Initialize method.

2. The body of the Timer Initialize method is shown in Figure 10.17. To create this body, follow these steps:

   A. You need to create a new parameter by clicking the Create New Parameter button and calling the parameter **AmountOfTime**. Make it a number.

   B. Select the World object from the object tree and select the Properties tab.

   C. Click the Create New Variable. Name this new variable **TimeLeft** and make it a number.

   D. Drag and drop the TimeLeft variable to the body of the method and set the variable to the AmountOfTime parameter.

3. Figure 10.18 shows how to create the body of the TimerCountdown method. To create this body, follow these steps:

   A. Drag and drop the While tile into the body of the method.

   B. Select the World object from the object tree and select the Functions tab.

   C. Scroll down for the A > B condition and drag and drop it over the True in the While condition. Set the parameters from the pop-up menu to TimeLeft and to 0.

   D. Set the text of the Timer object to the TimeLeft value.

Tip

This is where you have a numeric value that you need to convert to a string. The process is to select the 3D text object and drag its text property into the program. You can then assign the conversion of the numeric value to a string to the text property using the What as a string function (World object function).

   E. Drag and drop the Wait tile and select 1 Second.

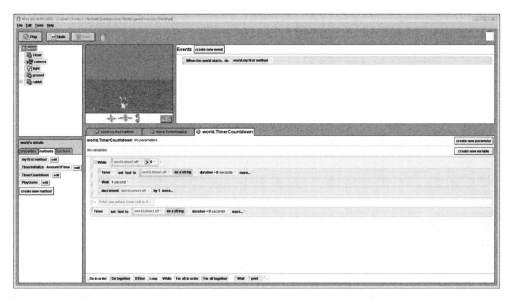

Figure 10.18
The TimerCountdown method.

   F.   Drag and drop the TimeLeft variable from the properties of the World
        object and select Decrement 1 from the pop-up menu.

   G.   After the While loop, set the text of the Timer object again as you did
        within the loop.

4. My First Method is used only for initializing the variable of the timer and
   initializing the variable that signals that the game is starting. The following
   creates the body of My First Method:

   A.   Select Properties for the World object.

   B.   Click the Create New Variable for the World properties. Name the
        variable **Start Game** and set it to the Boolean type.

   C.   Drag and drop the Start Game variable into the body and set it to True.

   D.   Select the Methods tab and drag and drop the World.TimerInitialize
        method to the body of the method above the Start Game setting.

Your method should resemble the method in Figure 10.19 when you have
completed these steps.

The next task is to fix the events part of this exercise. These events are playing the
game and the timer counting down. These two activities are done in parallel so

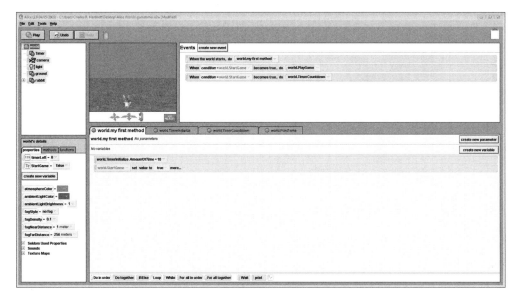

Figure 10.19
This is the completed program with events and My First Method.

that, as the users are playing the game, the timer is counting down. The Game Start variable being set to True triggers both of these events:

1. Click the Create New Event button and select When Something Becomes True. Do this twice.

2. Drag and drop the Game Start variable to the conditions for both events.

3. Click on the Nothing part of each event and select the Play Game and TimerCountdown methods appropriately, as seen in Figure 10.19.

4. Click on Play and watch the timer and the bunny hopping.

In this section, you completed a simple game that incorporates simple rules, collision detection, and scoring. This was a challenging task, but also a rewarding task. I hope that you also saw the process that I used to build this program. Firstly, the idea was created. Secondly, each function was built independently. Finally, you put all of the functions together to form the program.

Summary

The goal of this chapter was to show you how to implement scoring variables and timers. You first learned how to manipulate the 3D text object dynamically to support score keeping and timers. Secondly, you learned to keep the score in a simple game where the player tries to catch as many baseballs as possible. In the second example, you learned to implement a countdown timer as a part of a game or social networked virtual world. There are several ways that you can take the techniques in this chapter and build on them to suit the needs of your projects. Remember that it's a good idea to keep scoring as simple as possible so that you can determine whether the scoring is fair and useful. It is also important to keep in mind that your scoring needs to be accurate, and the more complicated the strategy, the more difficult it is to keep it accurate.

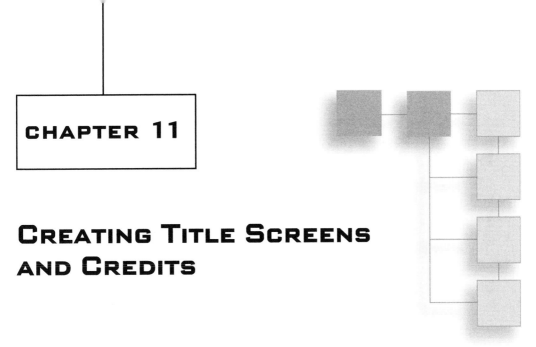

CHAPTER 11

CREATING TITLE SCREENS AND CREDITS

I am sure you have watched plenty of movies and shows on television and have noticed the title screens, captions, and ending credits. In addition, you will notice these same elements in video games and other forms of visual media. In this chapter, you will learn to implement various techniques for handling textual information on your screens. You will learn the various features of text in Alice, as well as how to fade text in and out, and other text animation techniques.

In this chapter, you can expect to see concepts that will help you do the following:

- Create, place, and format text on the screen

- Scroll text

- Fade in/out text

- Animate text

You will be revisiting the multiple-scene example from Chapter 8 at some point in this chapter and so if you have not completed that exercise or if you have misplaced it, you should be prepared to redo it. Let's get right to it!

Understanding the Basics of 3D Text

In Alice the text on the screen is rendered as 3D text. This means that the text has length, width, and depth just like the objects you have worked with throughout the text. Once you add 3D text to your world, it becomes an object like all other

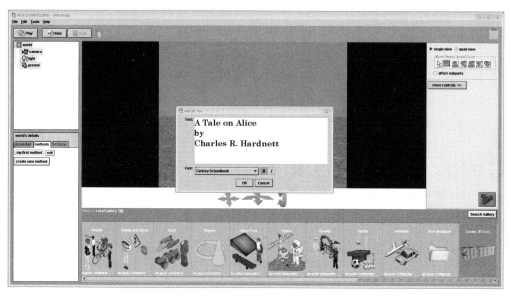

Figure 11.1
This shows the initial dialog box for adding text.

objects and can be controlled and manipulated in the same ways. The following instructions are the basics for adding text:

1. You must be in design mode and find the 3D text at the end of the gallery. Clicking it will provide a dialog box like the one shown in Figure 11.1.

2. Type some text that you want to see on the screen, such as your name or the title of your favorite movie or book.

   Formatting your text is like using many other software tools. There are icons for **bold** and *italics*. By selecting them, you can change the text in the dialog box.

   There is also a drop-down menu for the possible font selections. The fonts are the style for the text. Each time you select a font, the text in the dialog box will change as well.

3. After you have the text you want, click OK. Find the new object in the object tree and select it to look at its properties, as shown on the left side of Figure 11.2:

   A. **Extrusion:** The extension/stretching of the inner part of the font to provide the font more depth.

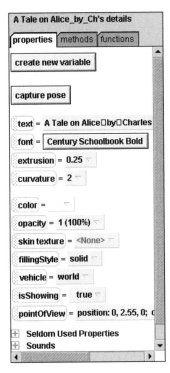

Figure 11.2
This figure shows the properties of a 3D text object.

B. **Curvature:** This refers to how much the characters are curved inward. For example, if the letter C is curved more, it will begin to touch and look like the letter O.

C. **Color:** The fill color for the characters.

D. **Opacity:** The degree of transparency. If set to 100%, there is no transparency. If set to 0%, there is complete transparency.

E. **Skin Texture:** This is used to load an image file that contains a patterned texture to be used for the text.

F. **Filling Style:** Determines how the text is drawn. The default is to draw the characters as if they were made of something solid like a block of wood. Other styles use a wireframe (skeleton) or just dots.

4. Make changes to any two of the properties and see how it changes the 3D text. The color and opacity are two of the easier properties to work with.

So far, you should have noticed that working with text in Alice is very similar to working with text in a word processor in some sense. In addition, you have the capabilities to program the text behaviors just like you programmed object behaviors before. This is the topic of the next section.

Using Fade In and Fade Out

Fade in and fade out are techniques that make the text slowly appear and slowly disappear. To properly perform these operations in a program, you must write the code that performs the operation. In this section, you learn to do a fade in, and after this you will be able to perform a fade out by reversing the logic.

Because the fade in and fade outs are operations describing the behavior of the text, these methods should belong to the text object. To do this, follow these steps:

1. Select the text in the object tree, and then select the Methods tab of the Details pane.

2. Click the Create New Method button and name the new method **FadeIn**.

3. Create another new method called **FadeOut**.

Figure 11.3 shows the result of the FadeIn method. Most of this type of code you have seen before. The part that is probably new to you is the portion of code that involves updating the Visible variable.

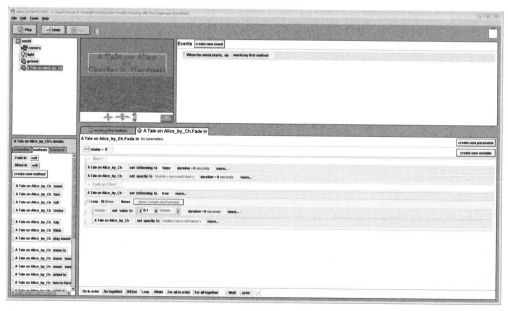

Figure 11.3
This shows the completed FadeIn method.

The basic idea for this code is the following:

- A fade in is where the text goes from being invisible (no opacity) to being solid (full opacity).

- A loop is needed to step from 0% opacity to 100% opacity.

The loop at the end of the program in Figure 11.3 is designed to increase the opacity from 0% to 100% in increments of 10%. The program starts by making the text invisible. Now, the loop is executed next and its purpose is to execute a fade in. The loop executes 10 times to accumulate 10% each time to reach 100%. At 100% the text is fully visible.

An accumulated sum is common in programming. It allows you to add a series of values together that are generated by a loop. Take the following algorithm as an example:

```
Set Foo to 0
Loop 10 times
    Set Foo to Foo + 1
End Loop
Print Value
```

The algorithm starts with the variable Foo set initially to 0. The loop will execute 10 times, but the important part here is the Set Foo to Foo + 1. The first Foo from the left will hold a new value. The second Foo represents the current value. The first time, Foo currently holds 0; therefore, Foo is equal to 0+1, which is 1. The second time through the loop, the current value of Foo is 1. Therefore, the new Foo is 1 + 1; where the first 1 is the value of Foo and the second 1 is from the Set statement in the loop. If you keep doing this, you will see that you will 1+1 to get 2, 2 + 1 to get 3, 3 + 1 to get 4, 4 + 1 to get 5, and so on, until 9 + 1 to get 10.

To create the accumulated sum for Visible, whereby the value of Visible is based on an older value of Visible, you have to do the following:

1. Open the FadeIn method by selecting the text object in the object tree, and then click the Edit button next to the FadeIn method name under the Methods tab.

2. Click the Create Variable button, and call the variable **Visible**. It should be initialized to 0 just like it is in Figure 11.3.

3. Select your 3D text object in the object tree and then click the Properties tab of the Details pane.

4. Drag and drop Is Showing into the program as shown in Figure 11.3. This should be set to False so that the text will disappear. Don't forget to set the duration to 0.

5. Drag and drop Opacity into the program, as shown in Figure 11.3. Don't forget to set the duration to 0.

These settings will ensure that the text does not show when the world starts. The duration of 0 is to make sure it happens without any delay.

6. Drag the Visible variable to the loop and set the value to 10. The next step will show the accumulation.

7. Using Figure 11.4, select the 10, and then follow the menu to Math, and select 10 +, and then select Expressions, and finally select Visible. The result will be an accumulation statement where 10 is being added to Visible and then stored back into Visible.

Now the new value of Visible will be based on the old value of Visible. This is the main idea behind the accumulation of the values being based on the sum of repeatedly adding 10%.

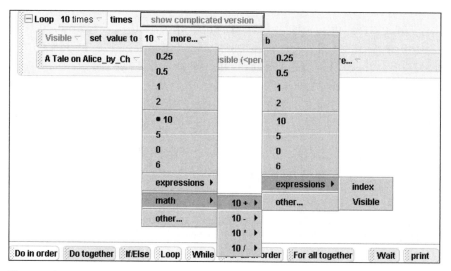

Figure 11.4
This figure shows how to do an accumulated sum on the variable Visible.

8. Open the My First Method by clicking on its tab in the editing pane, and drag the FadeIn method from the 3D text object into the body of the My First Method.

9. Now click the Play button.

If you have done everything properly, you should see the text appear slowly. That is a successful fade in. Creating a fade out involves essentially the same steps, but the Visible variable is initialized at 100% and then you subtract 10 each time. You have already created an empty method for the fade out. There is an example on the accompanying CD.

Using Zoom In and Zoom Out

The zoom in effect is where the text starts off far away from the camera, and then appears to be flying towards the camera until it is in perfect focus. The concept here is to create another method for your 3D text object and then place code into that method to perform the operation. The body for this method is shown in Figure 11.5. This method moves the text back 100 meters, which is far enough not to be seen. You can choose any value you would like to get the job done. Then the text is brought forward in a loop at 10 meters at a time.

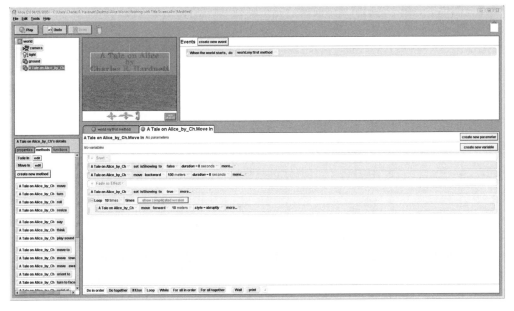

Figure 11.5
This figure shows the MoveIn method for the 3D text object.

Follow these steps to create the MoveIn method:

1. Select the 3D text object in the object tree, and then select the Methods tab in the Details pane.

2. Click the Create New Method button to create a method called **MoveIn**. This method will be used to hold the statements for moving/zooming in similar fashion as the FadeIn method.

3. Drag the Set Is Showing method and set it to False for the 3D text object into the function along with the Move method, with direction as Backward and distance as 100 meters. Ensure that both have a duration of 0 for instantaneous execution.

4. Drag a loop structure into the method and set it to execute 10 times.

5. Drag a Move method with a forward direction and 10 meters. Because this command is in the loop that will loop 10 times, the total distance moved is 10 * 10 meters = 100 meters.

6. Go to the My First Method of the World object, and drag the MoveIn method for the 3D text object. This requires you to select the World object in the object tree first to open the My First Method and then select the 3D text object in the object tree to get to the Move In method.

Of course, the zoom out effect is the opposite of the zoom in. It is interesting to note that although this effect was moving the text and the previous effect was changing a characteristic, they both have the loop in common. Why is that? The reason is that in both cases, there is the need to change a value over time.

Creating Scrolling Text

Scrolling text is based on the same idea that was used in the zooming example. However, there is a way that the zooming example and scrolling can be done without the use of the loop. This is due to the fact that Alice has methods that say "Move the object to a place or some distance". If you add a long duration to the method, you can have Alice say "Move the object some distance over some duration of time". Note that you have seen that *speed = distance/time* in your math classes. This is what you are using with these commands in Alice. By specifying the distance over some time period, you are determining how fast you want the object to move. In this case, you will use this to determine how fast the text scrolls.

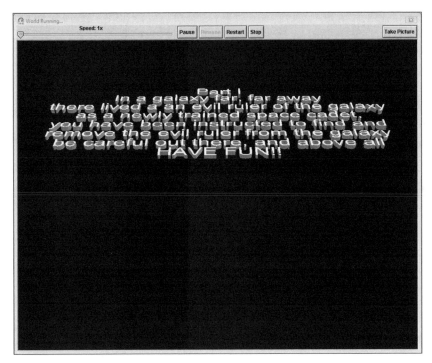

Figure 11.6
The text has been tilted back and is scrolling away into the darkness.

Instead of just scrolling the text upwards like you are probably thinking, I am going to show you an example where the text scrolls up at an angle like in the *Star Wars* movies. I thought that was always kind of cool and making Alice do it was even more fun.

In Figure 11.6, you can see the end result. This is surprisingly simple to do in Alice. To start, create a new project in Alice using the Space template.

Then you need to follow these steps:

1. Make the moon surface invisible. Select the Ground in the object tree and then, in the Properties tab, change the Is Showing value to False.

2. Add a 3D text object to your world with some text of your own. You can make it up or copy it from a book or website. You need to get about five to seven lines of text. Press the Return key between each line of text; otherwise, the text will not be on different lines.

3. In Figure 11.7, you will notice that the text is tilted backward. To do this, right-click the text in the object tree and, from Methods menu, choose

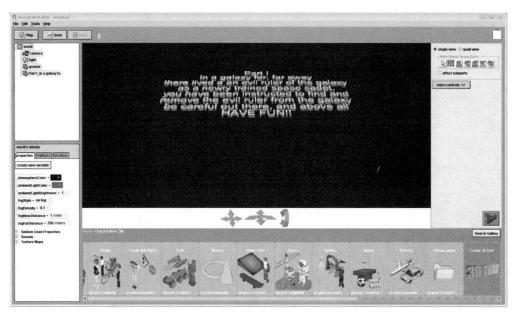

Figure 11.7
This shows the content and the initial position of the text for the *Star Wars*-like scroll.

Turn to Face and choose Camera. After that, use the toolbox Rotate Forward-Backward tool to rotate the worlds until they are at an angle similar to the one in the figure.

Figure 11.8 shows the body of the Scroll Away method. Create the method as a part of the 3D text object.

4. This code is very simple, but it does a lot. First, recognize that it moves the text down and then up. You probably thought it would have been forward and then backward. However, when you tilted the text backwards, its bottom is now facing you and its top is away from you. You move the text down at 0 duration to instantaneously hide the text when the world starts. Then move the text up, but move it slowly where it's covering 10 meters in 20 seconds. This will roughly give the viewer about 20 seconds to read the text as it scrolls by.

5. Drag the Scroll Away method into the My First Method body so that it will be started as the world starts.

6. Click Play to see the fabulous result!

That was very cool. In the next section, you will revisit the multi-scene program from Chapter 8 and add some transitional text, a title screen, and credits.

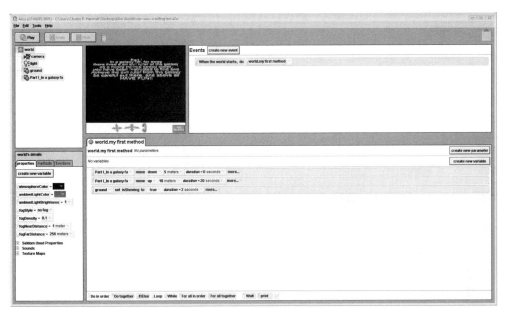

Figure 11.8
This shows the body of the method for scrolling away at an angle.

Adding Scene Headings

In Chapter 8, you developed a multi-scene virtual world example that had four scenes. The first scene was a pyramid, the second scene was a haunted house, the third scene is the football stadium, and the fourth scene is a city terrain. In this section, you are going to update this project with some of the text-manipulation ideas discussed in this chapter. You will add scene headings/titles for the four scenes and end it with some scrolling credits that have your name as the author, designer, and producer.

If you do not have your copy of this world, you can obtain it from the supplemental resources. This task is to integrate the fade in and zoom in techniques for all four scenes. This section will step you through part of the integration process and leave the remainder of the process as an exercise.

1. Create four 3D text objects to place into the four scenes with the appropriate titles, as shown in Figure 11.9.

    A. Use the Camera object and its Set Point of View method to point to the appropriate dummy objects.

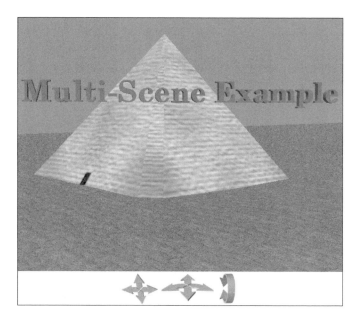

Figure 11.9
Shows the result of the first two scenes after the scene headings have been placed.

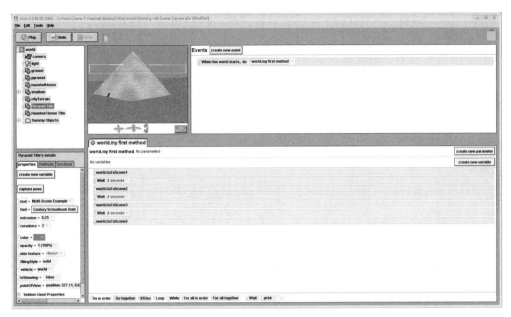

Figure 11.10
This shows the result of setting the Pyramid Text 3D Text object to not showing.

    B. Then add the 3D text object for that scene's heading.

    C. Now place the heading where you would want it to be.

2. Using Figure 11.10, set each of the 3D text objects' Is Showing property to False. In Figure 11.10, the Is Showing property for the Pyramid Text has been set. You do this by selecting the objects in the object tree and then going to the Properties tab in the Details pane.

3. Figure 11.11 shows how to call the pyramid text fade in method from within the Goto Scene 1 method. Use the same idea and use the zoom in method for the appropriate text object for some of the scenes and use the fade in for others.

4. Click Play and see the results.

This shows you how easy it is to have nice scene headings in your projects. You could extend this to have zoom out and fade out methods as well. For example, the fade out for the pyramid text used in scene 1 would be located in the Goto Scene 2 method before the point of view changes. You should spend some time working with these scene transitions and try different ideas.

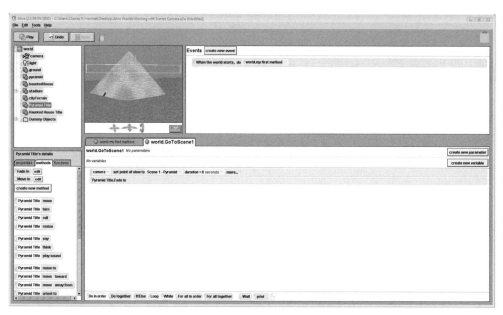

Figure 11.11
This figure shows you how to place a scene heading action into the scene setup method.

Summary

This chapter prepared you for developing nicer and more informative scene transitions. However, this chapter in general taught that you can manipulate text objects in the same way you manipulate other objects to animate them. These animated text objects are used to perform fade ins and fade outs, zoom ins and zoom outs, and scrolling, to name a few techniques. Use your imagination to take advantage of the programmability of text objects to create other interesting text manipulations in your projects. These exercises can be found on the accompanying CD.

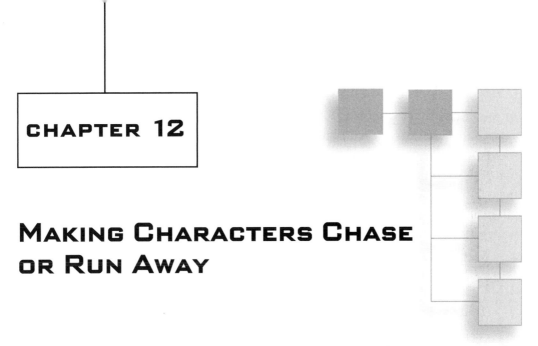

CHAPTER 12

MAKING CHARACTERS CHASE OR RUN AWAY

Artificial intelligence (A.I.) is where computer scientists work on giving computing device's intelligence. Most people associate A.I. with robots and androids because of what they see in the movies. However, A.I. is mostly about algorithms that can be turned into software and hardware to give computers intelligence. For example, A.I. scientists can study the organization of information to enable a machine to make connections between different pieces of information in order to allow the computer to make a decision. A.I. scientists also study how humans learn. The goal is to build algorithms that allow computers to learn in similar ways.

In virtual worlds, A.I. is used to give the computer-controlled characters decision-making skills to navigate the world autonomously. The goal is to make the computer-controlled character move through the virtual world with a program. The character could be searching for something as it moves around the world, or looking to attack the human-controlled character, or just patrolling some area to provide an obstacle or distraction for the human-controlled character. Pattern movement is the simplest way to automate the movements of computer-controlled characters. A pattern is preset pathway through the virtual world. The character is programmed to follow the pathway repeatedly. Chasing and evading are two classes of decision-making algorithms. *Chasing* is where a computer-controlled character is programmed to follow another character. *Evading* is where a computer-controlled character is running away from other characters, including any human-controlled characters. This chapter is about using chasing and evading strategies in your projects to make your characters more intelligent.

Using Algorithms to Simulate Intelligence

In previous chapters such as Chapters 3 and 5, you learned how to make characters move on the screen and move parts of their bodies. The user controlled the movements, or the computer controlled the movements. You learned how to make them walk and move their arms, and so on. With that knowledge, you can make a computer-controlled character walk around your world using a specified pathway or pattern. You can have a method that tells the character how far to walk and at what point to turn. For example:

1. Walk forward 10 meters.

2. Turn right one-quarter of a revolution.

3. Walk forward 10 meters.

4. Turn right one-quarter of a revolution.

5. Walk forward 10 meters.

6. Turn right one-quarter of a revolution.

7. Walk forward 10 meters.

The image in Figure 12.1 shows the result of the algorithm. An *algorithm* is a step-by-step set of instructions that can be the basis of a computer program. The algorithm starts by having the character walk forward 10 meters. If you start in

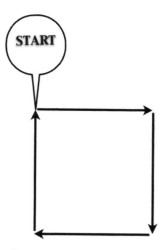

Figure 12.1
This figure shows the path taken by an object using the example algorithm.

the upper-left corner, the character can walk forward (to the right in the figure) and then turn right a quarter revolution. If the character turns right a quarter revolution, it is turning 90 degrees or at a right angle. This will cause your character to move along the path of the arrows in the figure.

Patterns like this are good for giving computer-driven characters the illusion of having intelligence. Although simple patterns like this box pattern are easy for a user to recognize, you can create more complex patterns that are harder for the user to recognize as patterns and that instead seem like actual intelligent movements.

However, patterns are not always the best choice. Sometimes, you want the characters to appear to follow or chase the user's character. In these cases, the computer-driven character needs more intelligence. For example, you can have an algorithm that is aware of the position of the user's character and move in that direction. For example:

1. Locate the position of the user's player.

2. Turn the computer-driven character to the player's position.

3. Move some distance forward and towards the player's position.

4. Go back and repeat Steps 1–3.

In this algorithm, the computer-driven character starts by determining where the player's character is located and then starts to move in that direction. Because the player is likely to move its character, the computer-driven character must relocate the position to chart a new path. This loop has to be done very quickly. This is because the user's player could be moving while your computer-driven character is making decisions and moves. Therefore, this algorithm needs to be processed as quickly as possible.

This algorithm provides some intelligence to your computer-driven character, and it will give the user the sense that the computer-controlled character is chasing the user's character. This is a very simple, but powerful way of adding intelligence. However, this type of algorithm has some flaws, depending on how you want to use it. Flaws include:

- What if there are obstacles in the scene and the character needs to navigate around them?

- What if there are other computer-controlled characters that need to be coordinated in their movements?

■ What if the computer-controlled character needs to collect some objects, such as weapons or special powers, as it moves around the world?

The following is an example algorithm where the computer-driven character could avoid objects:

1. Locate the position of the user's player.

2. Turn the computer-driven character to the player's position.

3. Move some distance forward and towards the player's position. If there is an obstacle in the pathway, turn to avoid the obstacle.

4. Go back and repeat Steps 1–3.

This is a simple approach to handling obstacles. When an obstacle is encountered in Step 3, the character finds a path around the obstacle. This can be as simple as just backing up and turning or just turning to another direction before going forward again; or it can be as complex as planning a new path and then following that path. You should always start with simpler approaches first and test the result; in many cases you will be satisfied with the results.

In the remainder of this chapter, you will see examples of these approaches. These examples are presented to give you a feel for how these algorithms should be implemented. You should realize that you may need to alter these algorithms for your own projects; don't be afraid to do that.

Making Characters Move in a Pattern

In this section, you will create a simple pattern for a character to follow while the world is running. Figure 12.2 shows that the pharaoh character should be initially set facing left in the scene. You will now create a pattern for the pharaoh to move on in the programming mode:

1. In Figure 12.3, note the method called Box Pattern. This method is created as a part of the Pharaoh object.

2. Drag a Loop tile into the body of the method.

3. Drag a Do In Order tile into the body of the Loop tile.

4. Drag the Move and Turn commands for the Pharaoh object into Do In Order.

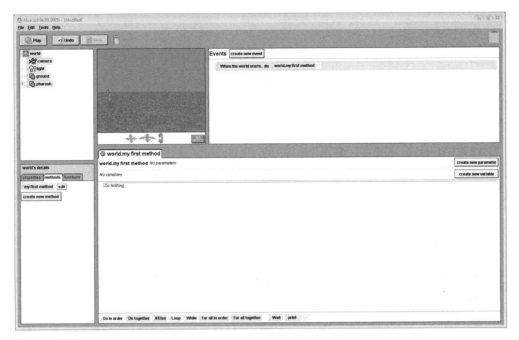

Figure 12.2
This figure shows the Pharaoh object at the start of the pattern.

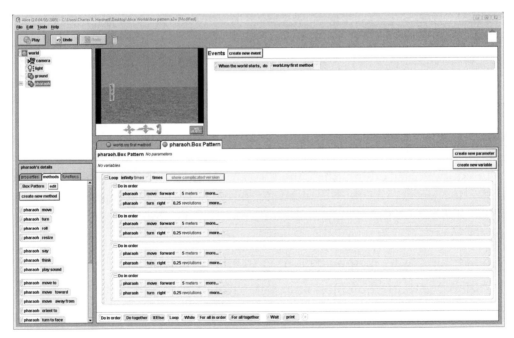

Figure 12.3
The function box pattern for the Pharaoh object.

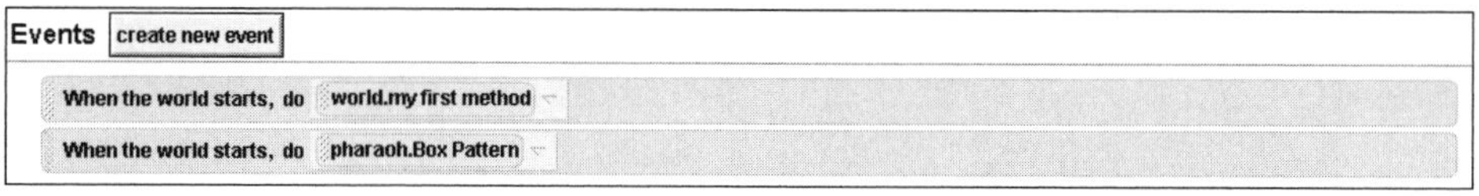

Figure 12.4
The new event for when the world starts to execute the box pattern.

5. Right-click on the edge of the Do In Order tile and select it to make a copy. Repeat this two more times so that you end up with four Do In Order tiles placed in the loop body.

6. Click on Create New Event and select When the World Starts. Drag the Box Pattern method for the Pharaoh object to this event. See Figure 12.4.

7. Click Play to see the result.

This example illustrates how to program a simple pattern. You can create your own pattern. It's best to first draw the pattern on a sheet of paper so that you can make sure the pattern is what you really want to convey; sketching first also helps better develop the actual moves and the turns. Next, determine where the turns are and the order of the turns. In between each turn, you will have a move forward. In this example, the move forwards were all the same length; however, in your pattern this may not be the case. Be creative with your patterns, and make them as interesting as you would like.

Chasing and Running Away

Earlier, you saw an example of chasing without accounting for obstacles. In this section, you will see how to create two effects: chasing and running away. These are just opposites of one another, and they are easily achieved in Alice. In order to create this program you will need to have a world that has two objects. Figure 12.5 shows the Bunny and Kangaroo objects. You can choose any two objects.

To build the chasing method, you need to follow these steps:

1. Select the Kangaroo object and click Create New Method. Call the new method **Chase Bunny**.

   The method shown in Figure 12.6 chases the bunny. This method is based on an infinite loop and follows the previous algorithm.

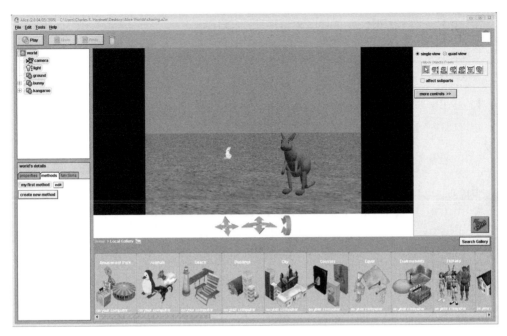

Figure 12.5
This shows the bunny and the kangaroo in the world.

Figure 12.6
This shows the Chase Bunny method.

2. Drag the Loop tile to the body of the method.

3. Drag the Turn to Face method for the Kangaroo object into the loop and have it face the Bunny object.

4. Drag the Move Forward method. You can use any distance you like and you might want to do some experimentation.

5. Click Play to see the result.

Now the Kangaroo object goes straight for the bunny. Next, you need to make the bunny move. You need to create Hop Forward and Hop Backward methods for the Bunny object. Then set up the Keyboard events using the example in Figure 12.7. After you have done this, click Play again and now you can move your bunny away.

Are you surprised at how easy that is? Alice provides you with several methods that can be used to chase and follow other characters. This is just one example of how to use some of these methods. So, what about running away? Since running away is the opposite of chasing, you can achieve that by changing one statement.

Figure 12.7
The Hop Forward method and the keyboard events.

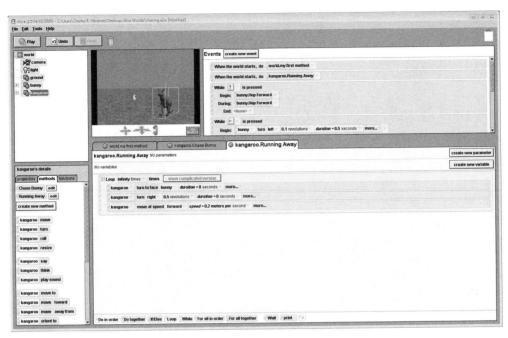

Figure 12.8
This shows the Running Away method, which you can accomplish by changing one statement of the previous method.

In Figure 12.8, the Running Away method is shown for the Kangaroo object. The change here is that you must add a statement that tells the Kangaroo to make a 180-degree (or half) rotation away from the bunny and then move forwards.

You can do all kinds of interesting things using this idea as your basis. Imagine having the kangaroo not just moving away from the bunny, but also moving towards another object. So when the kangaroo turns away, it turns to face the other object and then move towards it. You could also have the kangaroo make random movements to try to fake the bunny out. These are all fun ideas to play with.

Now you can see how to use some basic methods in Alice to build Chasing and Running Away methods for a computer-driven object. In the next section, you will build on this concept and teach the character to navigate obstacles.

Navigating Obstacles in a Path

When there are obstacles in the pathway of computer-driven character, there is more work to be done. Users could easily foil the current implementation if they simply stayed on the other side of an obstacle. This is because your

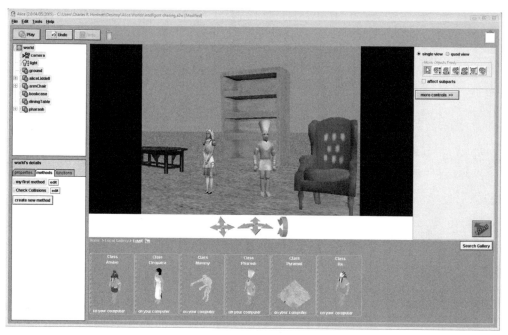

Figure 12.9
This figure shows the additions of the Pharaoh to the last exercise in Chapter 10.

computer-driven character only has one goal in mind: chase the user's character! Therefore, the solution is to take your one-track minded character and give it the ability to multitask. To do this, you will actually start with the same algorithm from the previous section, and you will need to open the world from Chapter 10 where you have Alice able to move around the bookshelf, table, and chairs. You can find this on the accompanying CD in the Chapter 10 folder if you do not have yours. If you have it, you can just open it, and then follow the instructions. Now, you are ready to follow these instructions:

1. Add the Pharaoh object to the world, as shown in Figure 12.9, and then return to the programming mode.

2. Now you need to modify the Detect Collision function by creating a new parameter called **Character**.

3. Drag and drop the new Character parameter over the reference to Alice in the IfElse tile. When you have finished, your modified function should look like the one in Figure 12.10.

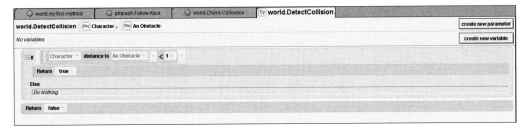

Figure 12.10
This figure shows the new Detect Collision function, which handles any character and any obstacle.

Figure 12.11
This figure shows the changes to the Check Collisions method.

4. Select the World object in the object tree, and then edit the Check Collisions method. Go to the object tree, and drag and drop the Alice object to the IfElse to replace the Character reference with Alice, as shown in Figure 12.11.

These steps have successfully converted the Detect Collision function to a function that does not depend on a particular character and obstacle as it did before. Because this function's parameters have changed, you also had to change the previous use of the function in the Check Collisions method. It calls the Detect Collision function that now needs to know which character to use. You will use the aliceLiddel character because this is the one you are controlling at the moment. At this time, the world should work the same as it did before, where Alice can be moved and bumped into the other objects.

1. Select the Pharaoh from the object tree and then click Create New Method. Create a new method called **Follow Alice**.

2. Build the Follow Alice method using the content shown in Figure 12.12. Start with putting the Loop tile into place. Then add the Turn to Look At

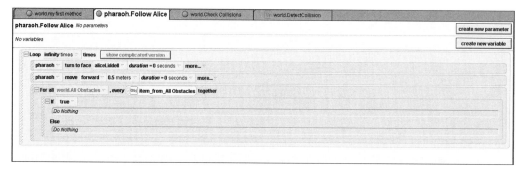

Figure 12.12
This figure shows the first part of the method that makes the Pharaoh follow Alice.

and the Move commands. Don't forget to adjust the durations on the commands to be 0 seconds.

3. Click and drag For All Together to the Loop tile and then select World.All Obstacles from the pop-up menu. Select An Obstacle from the expressions.

4. Click and drag the IfElse tile into the For All Together tile, and choose True.

5. Select the World object from the object tree and then choose the Functions tab.

6. Drag and drop the Detect Collisions function over True in the If Else tile. Select the Pharaoh and An Obstacle from the pop-up menu, as shown in Figure 12.13.

7. Place the Pharaoh Move Backward command below the condition for the first IfElse, as shown in Figure 12.14.

8. Drag and drop the IfElse tile to follow the previous command. This is the second IfElse tile for this method. This is also shown in Figure 12.14.

9. Select the World again, and this time drag and drop the Choose True Probability function to True in the new IfElse.

10. In Figure 12.15, the completed Follow Alice method is shown. Simply add the Turn Right, Turn Left, and Move Forward commands.

11. Also, create a new event for when the world starts and have it start the Follow Alice method.

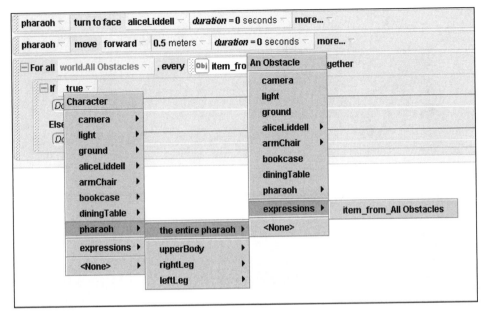

Figure 12.13
This figure shows the pop-up menu for the Detect Collision function.

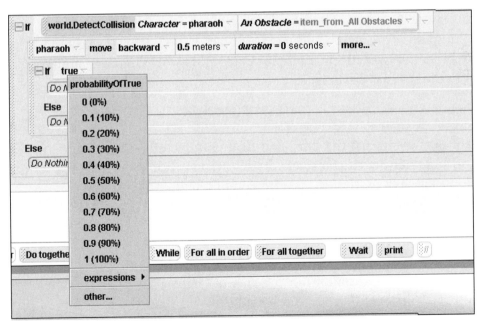

Figure 12.14
This figure shows the next stage of building this function.

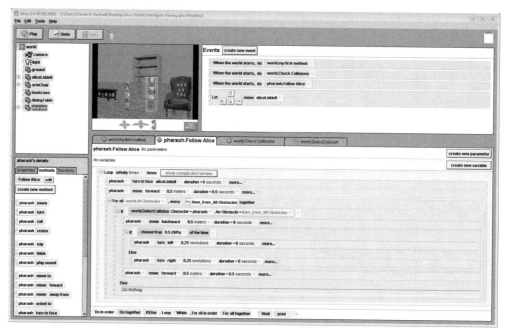

Figure 12.15
The completed Follow Alice method.

This last IfElse is used to make the computer-driven character turn left or right randomly to start avoiding the obstacle. This is not a foolproof way to do this, but it is an effective simple strategy that works in many simple game and virtual world circumstances.

12. Click Play to see how things are working!

You have now completed the third and final example of automating the movements of computer-driven characters. In this version, you have used the previous algorithm as a basis to develop a more complicated algorithm that enables the computer-driven character to become aware of obstacles and avoid them.

Summary

This chapter presents a topic from the area of artificial intelligence. There are many other algorithms that are more sophisticated than the ones I have presented here, but these are sufficient to give you a start in giving your characters some intelligence to navigate your virtual world. If you are interested in other strategies, you can look at sources for A.I. path-finding algorithm, tile-based path finding, continuous path finding, and flocking algorithms. The path finders are all focused on the same goal presented here: one computer-driven character chasing a user-controlled character. *Flocking algorithms* are where a collection of computer-driven characters works together in a coordinated way to follow another character or to reach a target. These concepts can be implemented in Alice but they are probably better suited for more advanced programming systems. There are examples of these systems and links on the website, which is located on the accompanying CD (www.spelman.edu/~hardnett/vworlds). Good luck with your future endeavors into A.I. techniques for following, chasing, evading, and running away!

INDEX

YOUR ULTIMATE RESOURCE

Course Technology PTR is your ultimate game development resource. Our books provide comprehensive coverage of everything from programming, story development, character design, special effects creation, and more, for everyone from beginners to professionals. Written by industry professionals, with the techniques, tips, and tricks you need to take your games from concept to completion.

NEW SERIES! Introducing the *GameDev.net Collection* series! Each book features a collection of the best articles taken from the GameDev.net archives, updated and revised for the current technology, as well as brand new articles never before published. GameDev.net is the leading online community for game developers to network and share ideas. Start your collection today!

Business and Production for Games
A GameDev.net Collection
1-59863-809-2 • $29.99

Design and Content Creation
A GameDev.net Collection
1-59863-808-4 • $49.99

Beginning Game Programming
A GameDev.net Collection
1-59863-805-X • $39.99

Advanced Game Programming
A GameDev.net Collection
1-59863-806-8 • $44.99

From Gamer to Game Designer
The Official Far Cry 2 Map Editing Guide
1-58450-686-5 • $39.99

Beginning OpenGL Game Programming
Second Edition
1-59863-528-X • $34.99

Character Animation with Direct3D
1-58450-570-2 • $39.99

Going to War
Creating Computer War Games
1-59863-566-2 • $34.99

Getting Started with Game Maker
1-59863-882-3 • $34.99

Game Programming with Silverlight
1-59863-906-4 • $39.99

Introduction to Game Development
Second Edition
1-58450-679-2 • $49.99

ShaderX7
Advanced Rendering Techniques
1-58450-598-2 • $59.99

Behavioral Mathematics for Game AI
1-58450-684-9 • $49.99

Game Coding Complete
Third Edition
1-58450-680-6 • $59.99

Protecting Games
A Security Handbook for Game Developers and Publishers
1-58450-670-9 • $39.99

Beyond Game Design
Nine Steps Toward Creating Better Videogames
1-58450-671-7 • $39.99

David Perry on Game Design
A Brainstorming Toolbox
1-58450-668-7 • $49.99

COURSE TECHNOLOGY
CENGAGE Learning

Professional • Technical • Reference

Our complete line of books is available at Amazon Barnes & Noble, Borders, and other fine retailers nationwide. Visit us online at **www.courseptr.com** or call **800-354-9706**

You're a teen with a great imagination...

Written specifically for teens in a language you understand, on topics you're interested in! Each book in the *For Teens* series features step-by-step instructions to help you conquer the tools and techniques presented. Hands-on projects help you put your new skills into action. And the accompanying CD-ROM or web downloads provide tutorials, instructional videos, software programs, and more!

...unleash your creativity with the  series!!

Computer Programming for Teens
ISBN: 1-59863-446-1 • $29.99

Web Comics for Teens
ISBN: 1-59863-467-4 • $29.99

3D Game Programming for Teens
ISBN: 1-59200-900-X • $29.99

Game Creation for Teens
1-59863-500-X • $29.99

Torque for Teens
ISBN: 1-59863-409-7 • $29.99

Web Design for Teens
ISBN: 1-59200-607-8 • $19.99

**Microsoft Visual Basic
Game Programming for Teens**
Second Edition
ISBN: 1-59863-390-2 • $29.99

Game Art for Teens
Second Edition
ISBN: 1-59200-959-X • $34.99